Knowledge and Learning in Organizations

Fabiano Larentis · Claudia Simone Antonello

Knowledge and Learning in Organizations

A Knowing-In-Practice Perspective of University
Academic Managers

Fabiano Larentis
Management Graduate Program
Universidade de Caxias do Sul
Caxias do Sul, Rio Grande do Sul
Brazil

Claudia Simone Antonello
Department of Administrative
Sciences
Universidade Federal do Rio Grande
do Sul
Porto Alegre, Rio Grande do Sul
Brazil

ISBN 978-3-031-61166-7   ISBN 978-3-031-61167-4   (eBook)
https://doi.org/10.1007/978-3-031-61167-4

This Palgrave Macmillan imprint is published by the registered company Springer Nature Switzerland AG
The registered company address is: Gewerbestrasse 11, 6330 Cham, Switzerland

If disposing of this product, please recycle the paper.

PREFACE

This book is about universities, their complexities, and dynamics, specifically university management. It is about a special agent in this context, who is fundamental for the university processes, strategies, outcomes, and sustainability. It is about the academic manager, the one who works at university management, either temporarily or permanently, without abandoning the identity as a professor. The one that is supposed to deal with the balance between teaching, researching, and managing.

We present and deepen in this book the findings of a research study we developed in southern Brazil, in a community university. The research, a qualitative study, was performed by Professor Fabiano Larentis (University of Caxias do Sul) in his post-doctorate, advised by Professor Claudia Simone Antonello (Federal University of Rio Grande do Sul). Its purpose was to analyze the configuration of academic managers' knowing, taking into account the knowing-in-practice notion as theoretical and analytical lenses.

It is necessary to mention that knowing goes beyond knowledge. Symbolically it is a transition from a noun to a verb, since knowledge is considered as a process and a collective activity in situated contexts—it goes beyond the generation and transmission of knowledge. Knowing is knowledge as an activity that itself constitutes practice. It is therefore about learning as a social and cultural phenomenon, not just cognitive and individual, stressing the role of human action in complex organizational work.

Why the interest about academic managers? Besides the importance to investigate this agent and the research gaps about this topic, detailed in the first chapter, we have had experiences as academic managers in our paths as professors and researchers in Management. We have realized in practice how complex and interesting managing a university is, in its diverse hierarchical levels, structures, relationships, and operations, with its traditions, challenges, and idiosyncrasies. As researchers specially in the theme Learning in Organizations, our practice has provoked us to explore and to deepen the way the academic manager's role and knowing are accomplished.

Lastly our research proposes a framework, which we nominate as "The cauldron of knowing of the academic manager", in which a culinary metaphor is associated to the academic manager's path entangled with aspects of the situated context. The book is the opportunity to explore this framework and recommend some guidelines, serving not only researchers interested in university and university management, but also practitioners at HEI, in their diverse formats.

We thank our spouses, sons, and daughters, as well as some university colleagues, for encouraging the development of this book. Also, we are grateful to the National Council for Scientific and Technological Development (CNPq) for the financial support. Lastly, we appreciate the invaluable support of both Marcus Ballenger and Geetha Chockalingam, our editorial team at Palgrave Macmillan Publisher, since they first proposed to elaborate a book based on a research carried out in Brazil. Thank you for the indispensable observations and recommendations to make this project possible.

Caxias do Sul, Brazil   Fabiano Larentis
Porto Alegre, Brazil   Claudia Simone Antonello

CONTENTS

About the Authors

Fabiano Larentis obtained his Doctor in Management from the Federal University of Rio Grande do Sul (BR). He is a Professor at the Management Graduate Program, University of Caxias do Sul (UCS), Caxias do Sul (BR). He researches themes associated to learning in organizations and people management. He is Vice-Chancellor at University of Caxias do Sul—Campus Bento Gonçalves (BR)

Claudia Simone Antonello obtained her Doctor in Management from the Federal University of Rio Grande do Sul (BR). She is a Professor at the Management Graduate Program, Federal University of Rio Grande do Sul (UFRGS). She researches themes associated to learning in organizations and practice-based studies.

LIST OF TABLES

CHAPTER 1

Introduction: Becoming an Academic Manager—A Knowing-in-Practice Perspective

Abstract Universities have a complex and dynamic nature. Its management depends on an important position, the academic manager, the one who manages without abandoning the teaching identity. However, how does the constitution process of the academic manager take place, involving learning and knowing? In this chapter we focus on the main elements related to the configuration of academic managers' knowing, taking the theoretical and analytical lens of the knowing-in-practice perspective. Concepts related to university management, practice, knowing-in-practice, academic manager, and academic manager knowing and learning are provided. Details about the qualitative study that grounds this book are indicated, such as the data collection and analysis procedures, mostly the categorization process that supports the development of the framework, named The Cauldron of Knowing of the Academic Manager.

Keywords Learning · Knowing · Knowing-in-practice · University management · Academic manager · Community university

Universities are peculiar organizations. Grounded on the values of academic freedom and autonomy, their level of complexity involves not just aspects related to education, but also research, innovation, and

F. Larentis and C. S. Antonello, *Knowledge and Learning in Organizations*, https://doi.org/10.1007/978-3-031-61167-4_1

1

human development, in other words, knowledge creation and sharing, with their effects on societies. Moreover, universities are associated to the development of regions in several ways. However, their social and economic contexts provide continual unpredictability (Al Mahameed et al., 2024; Davis et al., 2016; Geschwind et al., 2019b; Johnson, 2002; Krücken et al., 2013; Mattsson et al., 2023).

Due to their millennial paths, universities are supposed to balance the relationship between tradition, knowledge quality, and their sustainability, not only in an economic way. Their traditional organizational structures, the levels and weight of bureaucracy, the processes, and the academic freedom have been challenged, mainly when we consider university effectiveness, which means the use of resources and the achievement of diverse goals. Also, their increasingly volatile external and institutional contexts throughout the world embraces declining state funding, changing students' demographics, technological advancements, and market pressures (Al Mahameed et al., 2024; Davis et al., 2016; Frenkel, 2021; Geschwind et al., 2019b; Hess, 2023; Johnson, 2002; Johnson & Deem, 2003; Loveday, 2021; Mattsson et al., 2023; Winter, 2017).

University management has been under scrutiny. Words and expressions such as audit, market goals, customer needs, student's satisfaction, society needs, usefulness of research results, access to resources, optimization, marketization, corporatization, work precariousness, sustainability, and managerialism have been present in narratives, intentions, decision-making, and practices from several publics, such as companies and entrepreneurs, researchers, governments and NGOs (Al Mahameed et al., 2024; Davis et al., 2016; Deem & Brehony, 2005; Geschwind et al., 2019b; Hess, 2023; Loveday, 2021; Mattsson et al., 2023; Winter, 2017).

In such aspect, it is important to pay attention to the role of managerialism, since it has the potential to solve inefficiencies in university systems, in the same way that has generated disempowered middle managers, an over-articulation of strategy, a culture of conformance over collegiality, a short-term vision jeopardizing long-term scientific advances, and control at the cost of innovation (Davis et al., 2016; Geschwind et al., 2019a; Hess, 2023; Mattsson et al., 2023). Researchers mainly from sociology, education, and organization studies, such as those beforementioned in this chapter, have addressed several constraints and concerns about the dynamic of management and organizational structures in university contexts, including the role, responsibilities, and development of the academic manager.[1]

This book is about academic managers' knowing, in a scenario of complex dynamics, processes, and structures, regarding universities and their management. Specifically, we focus on the configuration of academic managers' knowing, taking the knowing-in-practice notion as theoretical and analytical lens. First of all, we present some definitions and features associated to the academic manager. Afterwards, we deepen the concepts of practice and the knowing-in-practice notion.

Working in a university means high scientific level and specific management aspects in a scenario of restricted access to resources and external competition (Bessant & Mavin, 2016; Broadbent, 2011; Iorga, 2011; Jones & Weinrib, 2022). In this scenario, we highlight the role of the academic manager, the one who acts in higher education management, either temporarily or permanently, without abandoning the teaching identity (Barbosa et al., 2018; Castro & Tomàs, 2011; Ésther, 2011).

The academic manager position is associated to the multiplicity of roles exercised, the presence of relationship with various publics, the temporariness in the position, the relevance to mediate the path and rhythm of change, the lack of preparation for management positions, the unpredictability of the agenda of activities, time management, and work overload, which is intensified by information technology. We also have the relationship with people who do not properly value administrative activities and succession challenges (Barbosa et al., 2016a, 2016b, 2017; Broadbent, 2011; Dowling-Hetherington, 2014; Martin, 2022; Rodrigues & Villardi, 2017; Silva, 2012; Silva & Cunha, 2015).

It is important to mention that the competences required for management are intrinsic and distinct from other university activities (Barbosa et al., 2016a). Moreover, there is a duality in interpersonal relationships, with moments of aggregation and pleasure and moments of conflict and tension (Silva, 2012).

The multiple activities of the academic manager's encompass the challenge of reconciling teaching, research, and management activities, including boundaries outside the university (Broadbent, 2011;

---

[1] We also have the use of the term "manager-academic" in such situations, as in Johnson (2002), Deem and Johnson (2003), Deem and Brehony (2005), and Loveday (2021). We opted for the term "academic manager", due to its greater prevalence in scientific studies, taking in consideration the focus presented here.

Geschwind et al., 2019a; Iorga, 2011; Silva, 2012). There is a need to navigate between traditional academic values, managerialist pressures, and their academic and manager identities (Frenkel, 2021; Machovcová et al., 2019).

We still have to consider the transitoriness of the academic manager activity. As mentioned by the study of Silva and Cunha (2015), this element involves the loss of power, the feeling of persecution, people's change of interest in the relationship (scantiness of opportunism), and the managers' view even after the transition, which is entitled the ex-manager syndrome: the manager identity remains. The family plays a significant role in this transition.

In turn, when academic managers are contemplated as a social group, they are interested in keeping relations of power and domination, in a context of work contradictions and tensions, mainly those linked to managerialism and collegiality (Clegg, 2003; Deem & Brehony, 2005; Geschwind et al., 2019a; Jones & Weinrib, 2022; Winter, 2009). The focus on context is central, regarding interpersonal, political, and ethical focuses (Barbosa et al., 2016a; Bessant & Mavin, 2016; Machovcová et al., 2019).

Academic managers are supposed to deploy diverse capabilities, which are dependent on contingencies. Such capabilities become effective when they are translated into action in practice, recognized by the subject and by third parties (Barbosa et al., 2018). Additionally, the path as academic manager emphasizes the importance of teamwork and interpersonal relationships, how to deal with mistakes, conflicts, and different worldviews, and the emergence of lasting friendships (El-Awad et al., 2022; Silva, 2012). In this respect, academic manager learning is believed to be gradual, since one experiences incremental involvement in management, situated in contexts as a product of practice, dialogue, and critical reflection (Johnson, 2002), which lead us to the concepts of practice and knowing-in-practice.

Learning and knowledge are mostly social and cultural phenomena (Gherardi, 2015; Nicolini et al., 2003; Silva & Larentis, 2022). As organizational studies advance in understanding subjectivity and intersubjectivity, tacit and aesthetic elements, new ontological, epistemological, theoretical, and methodological contributions are required (Gherardi, 2006, 2019, 2021). From this standpoint, the notion of practice means a differentiated way to think about social research in organizations (Gherardi, 2006; Nicolini et al., 2003). Elements such as human activity, knowledge, meaning, language, organizations, power, and technological and historical transformations take place and are components of the field of practices (Nicolini et al., 2003). Practices are the ways of doing of a society, which emerge from the entanglement of doing and knowing, since heterogeneous items are ordered and performed into a coherent whole. They are related to social construction and reproduction, in which discursive actions and materials acquire meaning, stabilized and legitimized through repetition of activities (Gherardi, 2001, 2006, 2009; Nicolini, 2012). Based on this, knowing is a situated way of knowledge and acting, directed by the world of senses (Gherardi, 2009).

As specified by Gherardi (2019), firstly practices create encoded situations encompassing programs of action, but there is no compulsoriness as to how actions shall be performed. Secondly, the distinction of working practices is not in their internal variability, but in their repetition. Practices entail elements of action but are not actions. For example, evacuating from a fire is action for residents and practice for firefighters. The third characteristic is that practice reproduces society.

The symbolic transition from knowledge (noun) to knowing (verb) prepares the way for a view of knowledge as a process and a collective activity, more performative than cognitive (Bruni et al., 2007; Gherardi, 2006; Hopwood, 2014). Therefore, the knowing-in-practice notion emerges, which stresses the role of human action in complex organizational work in situated contexts, in social structures that are both the context and production of human activities (Bruni et al., 2007; Orlikowski, 2002; Scaratti et al., 2009).

As a process that results in knowledge, knowing goes beyond the generation and transmission of knowledge and it is a social condition for learning a practice (Nicolini et al., 2003). It cannot be seen as a conscious activity involving meaningful acts, since it presupposes only presumed or indirect references to meanings, values, and norms (Gherardi, 2008).

Knowing can also be perceived as knowledge accomplished through activity. In other words, knowing-in-practice, since knowledge is an activity that itself constitutes practice, making connections in action in the historical, social, and cultural context in which it unfolds, bearing in mind the work practices performed by humans and non-humans, also known as sociomateriality (Bruni et al., 2007; Gherardi, 2006, 2009; Gherardi & Perotta, 2014; Hopwood, 2014). Sociomateriality is related to the materiality of knowing and non-human actants (objects, tools, artifacts, spaces, texts, discourses, technology) through the senses (Gherardi, 2006, 2019). Doing is never without objects: practices comprehend material and social doing (Nicolini, 2012).

Within this context, Lee and Amjadi (2014) mention that knowing-in-practice contemplates the nature of knowledge on four axes: (a) knowledge is emergent, generated from daily activities; (b) knowledge is embodied, dependent on the physical presence and experience of people; (c) knowledge is rooted in the historical-cultural context; (d) knowledge is material, related to various objects, physical contexts, spaces, and infrastructure.

However, why do the topics academic managers and the knowing-in-practice notion deserve to be investigated and explored?

It is necessary to mention that learning and knowing in organizations discussed in the Practice-Based Studies (PBS) takes the practices within the context of organizations as the locus for investigating learning. As a consequence, they present the potential to handle organizational complexity in a suitable way, filling gaps in the studies developed on this subject (Durante et al., 2019; Gherardi, 2006; Price et al., 2020). Practice-based approaches allow to dissolve the separations between different levels of learning and overcome conceptual dualities, thus contributing to the advancement of organizational studies focused on learning and knowing (Antonello & Godoy, 2010; Chia, 2017; Cuel, 2020; Elkjaer, 2022; Gherardi, 2015; Price et al., 2020).

With this book we will have an opportunity to adopt and deepen the knowing-in-practice notion in order to comprehend how academic managers' knowing is constituted in the light of their socio-historical context, based on the findings of a research performed in a community university. On account of its placing in social practice, knowing-in-practice means that knowing implies a processual understanding of the capability for action, as they constantly are connected and reconnected. Knowledge emerges from the context of its production and is anchored by material bases.

This book addresses practice-based approaches, which allow us to dissolve the separations between different levels of learning and prevail over conceptual dualities, thus enabling the advancement of organizational studies (Antonello & Godoy, 2010; Cuel, 2020; Durante et al., 2019; Elkjaer, 2022; Gherardi, 2015). As underscored by Price et al. (2020), a practice-based approach does not reinforce the study of managers as individuals or collectives, neither learning or education as detached activities, but rather the study of the social and material effects of their interconnections.

Furthermore, it is quite timely to study higher education organizations and actors with a management focus. Also, we have a political and professional complexity that highlights the proper focuses of the practice and knowing-in-practice, which deals with a complexity that reduces the explanatory power of traditional categories of organizational analysis (Barbosa et al., 2017; Frenkel, 2021; Loveday, 2021; Protasio & Tauchen, 2021; Rodrigues & Villardi, 2017).

The book deepens and enhances the comprehension of the constitution process of the academic manager in HEI, within the perspective of knowing-in-practice. We provide a relevant and opportune understanding of the learning processes related to the academic managers, the multiplicity of roles, problems, decisions, conflicts, and worldviews, the diverse levels of preparation, the political and power aspects, the relationship to various publics, and the temporariness of the position. Other studies associated to academic managers often focus on the development of capabilities and their role in university management (Barbosa et al., 2016a, 2016b, 2017; Bessant & Mavin, 2016; Broadbent, 2011; Castro & Tomàs, 2011; El-Awad et al., 2022; Ésther, 2011; Frenkel, 2021; Iorga, 2011; Jones & Weinrib, 2022; Loveday, 2021; Machovcová et al., 2019; Martin, 2022; Protasio & Tauchen, 2021; Rodrigues & Villardi, 2017; Silva & Cunha, 2015; Winter, 2009).

In addition to the research and managerial gaps mentioned before, it is crucial to comment that we have demonstrated interest in this topic due to our paths and experiences as professors and academic managers in two different kinds of universities in Brazil, community and public federal.

The author Fabiano Larentis obtained this PhD title (Management) from a Public Federal University (Federal University of Rio Grande do Sul), and has been a professor in a non-profit community university (University of Caxias do Sul) since 2006, working with undergraduate courses, a graduate program (Management), and developing research. Also, he has experiences as academic manager since 2012, working as coordinator in undergraduate and graduate programs, coordinator in pro-rectory in support of the vice-chancellor, and lastly as vice-chancellor in the second most important campus.

The author Claudia Simone Antonello obtained this PhD title (Management) from Federal University of Rio Grande do Sul, where she has been a professor since 2008, working with undergraduate courses, a graduate program (Management), and developing research. She has experience as academic manager since 2011 as coordinator in a graduate program. The book is based on a research study we performed in a Community University located in southern Brazil, State of Rio Grande do Sul (University of Caxias do Sul/UCS—https://www.ucs.br/site/eng lish/).

We developed a qualitative study through a praxiography, a practice-based ethnography (Gherardi, 2015, 2019), which assumes practice as an epistemology that decenters the human subject and enables it to focus on how humans, discourses, and materialities achieve agency by entangling themselves with practice. The data collection comprehended 47 semi-structured interviews, resulting in 51 hours, 288 hours of participant observation, and 16 documents. The research was registered in the university ethics committee via "Plataforma Brasil".

The field of study was a multi-campus community university located in southern Brazil—University of Caxias do Sul (UCS), and took into account the practices of its academic managers. This institution was founded more than 55 years ago and it is located in a region with 1 million inhabitants (Serra Gaúcha), recognized by its diversified economy and a culture influenced mainly by the Italian immigration. UCS has around 21 thousand undergraduate and graduate students, as well as research and innovation activities. This institution is considered one of the best community universities in Brazil, according to the QS Ranking Latin America. As a non-profit community university, it is classified as a plural organization, a term used by Mintzberg (2015) to describe those that are neither public nor private, with a particular focus on communities and an emphasis on purpose. According to him, the plural sector is about shared communityship, while the private sector is about individual ownership and the public sector is about collective citizenship.

The interviews were recorded and transcribed, with the texts forwarded for validation by the interviewees. The interviewees were 17 coordinators, 8 knowledge area directors, 5 campus directors, 5 rectory members, 2 former managers in rectory position and nowadays acting as professors, 5 former managers in rectory and retired, and 5 non-professor employees subordinated to academic managers.

We worked with a semi-structured script and the projective technique of interview to the double (Gherardi, 2019), which focused on professional trajectory, role played as academic manager, relation with management tools and technology, and university relationships. Regarding the interviews with employees subordinated to the academic managers in activity, another semi-structured script was used by adapting the same themes of the script for academic managers.

One of the researchers was responsible for the participant observation, involving interactions with academic managers and employees during six months, such as meetings and informal moments, resulting in a field diary. The observations were focused on the way in which the experiences and acquired knowledge could be evidenced.

When we consider the document research, the 16 documents used were associated to the university strategic and institutional planning and, the work instructions and procedures of conduct for academic managers, such as information systems' instructions. pedagogic plans, guidelines to academic coordinators, and councils' rules of conduct.

For data analysis, we followed the criteria of thematic analysis (Braun & Clarke, 2014), which does not seem to contradict the assumptions of practice-based studies focusing on knowing-in-practice. This type of analysis was chosen because it is an accessible, flexible method capable of handling both small and large databases in qualitative studies. NVIVO software was used in order to support the organization of the data. The analysis considered 6 phases: (a) familiarization with the data; (b) initial codes generation; (c) searching for themes; (d) themes review; (c) themes definition; (e) report elaboration. We emphasize that this process was not linear, requiring a recursive attitude, with back-and-forth movements as necessary.

The coding process was a posteriori. We generated a total of 277 codes which, when grouped together, allowed for the constitution of what we call microcategories, in a total of 43. We observe that these microcategories were not intended to fragment the findings: this organization had the purpose to highlight where certain elements predominated, although they may also be present in more than one context of analysis.

The 43 microcategories were organized into 9 analytical categories: connecting to management, maturing as a manager, disconnecting from management, dealing with structure and processes, dealing with oneself, dealing with the nature of the academic and manager relationship, dealing with power, dealing with external connections, and dealing with internal connections. Some microcategories were shared between categories. We reinforce that the use of the gerund in the denomination of most microcategories and analytical categories is due to the focus on the notion of knowing-in-practice.

According to the main research findings, knowing is configured as the academic manager connects to management, matures as a manager, and disconnects from management, in interaction with individual, social, relational, structural, sociomaterial, and political aspects, intertwined when dealing with the nature of the academic manager relationship. We highlight the consideration of practices and knowing-in-practice regarding academic manager's social practices, performed in time and space, in situation and context. Therefore, in a knowledge-intensive context such as the university, social action and knowledge can be considered as inseparably intertwined activities (Gherardi, 2009). The constitution of the academic manager has been identified as involving reproduction of society and the practice as productive of its effects. In the book, we deepen the forementioned research findings, focusing on the implications to university management and on the role of the academic manager.

In the context studied, we highlight academic managers conceiving and perceiving themselves in a diversity of internal and external (dis)connections, including the professors as subordinates and colleagues. In this sense, the work practices performed by humans and non-humans encompass a complex network between people, material artifacts, activities, ideas, and information (Bruni et al., 2007; Gherardi, 2009, 2019; Orlikowski & Scott, 2015).

These aspects are synthesized in a framework, derived from the research findings and inspired by gastronomy as metaphor, entitled "The cauldron of knowing of the academic manager", in which its elements are part of food in a broth, due to the processual and interactive nature of the knowing-in-practice notion. These elements will compose the book chapters. The framework was created based on the 43 microcategories and the 9 analytical categories identified in the study, formerly indicated: connecting to management, maturing as a manager, disconnecting from management, dealing with structure and processes, dealing with oneself, dealing with the nature of the academic and manager relationship, dealing with power, dealing with external connections, and dealing with internal connections. Both the microcategories and analytical categories are presented in the framework.

Therefore, this book, in particular the proposed framework and its elements, which will compose the chapters, enables a better understanding and evidencing of the role of the university academic manager, with the notion of knowing-in-practice. In the next chapter, "The cauldron of knowing of the academic manager", we briefly develop the elements that are part of the conceptual framework that emerged from the research findings, the cauldron. We deepen the culinary analogy regarding the academic-manager's knowing and present the way the framework's elements are connected, as well as the dynamic behind these connections. We take into account the way the academic manager develops and the implications to university management.

In Chapter 3, "Academic manager's Path: From Connections to Disconnections", we deepen the following elements of the cauldron: Maturing as a manager; Connecting to management; Disconnecting from management; Transitions Zones; Dealing with oneself. These parts are in the center of the cauldron. We present managerial implications for aspects such as previous experiences, connections before management, learning through pain and mistakes, interacting with information systems and management methodologies, knowing through reflection, sharing and dialoguing, dealing with time, dealing with humility and emotions, concerns about succession, managing to detach, and dealing with the return to teaching.

Chapter 4 encompasses the "Contextualizing Elements of Academic managers' Knowing". Connected with the previous chapters, we work with the following elements of the cauldron: Dealing with structure and processes; Dealing with power; Dealing with external connections; and Dealing with internal connections. We present managerial implications for aspects such as dealing with hierarchy and processes, dealing with the authority of the position, meanings arising from physical spaces, dealing with conflicts, dealing with non-academic managers and support sectors, relating to the teams, amplitude, and quality of external connections, and dealing with graduates, the communities and other stakeholders.

In Chapter 5, "Constituting oneself as an Academic manager: Nature, opportunities, Challenges and Guidelines", the cauldron's category "Dealing with the nature of the academic and manager relationship" is developed, whose results will be related to the previous chapters. We consider aspects such as teaching contributing to management and vice-versa, research contributing to management, and the weight of the interaction between manager and professor. Within this context, we present opportunities, challenges, and guidelines regarding academic managers' constitution of skills, attitudes, and behaviors, in formal and informal learning contexts.

Taking into consideration that management practices should not only focus on what managers "do", but also on the consequences of their "doing" (Price et al., 2020), in the last chapter, "Concluding Remarks", we end the book with some theoretical and managerial implications. The importance and the challenges of the academic manager role to university management are emphasized.

REFERENCES

Al Mahameed, M., Yates, D., & Gebreiter, F. (2024). Management as ideology: "New" managerialism and the corporate university in the period of Covid-19. *Financial Accountability & Management, 40*(1), 34–57. https://doi.org/10.1111/faam.12359

Antonello, C. S., & Godoy, A. S. (2010). The crossroads of organizational learning: A multiparadigmatic view. *Revista de Administração Contemporânea, 14,* 310–332. https://doi.org/10.1590/S1415-65552010000200008

Barbosa, M. A. C., Matos, F. R. N., Mendonça, J. R. C., Paiva, K. C. M., & Cassundé, F. R. de S. A. (2017). The role of manager: Perceptions from academic managers of a Brazilian Federal University. *Education Policy Analysis Archives, 25,* 12. https://doi.org/10.14507/epaa.25.2388

Barbosa, M. A. C., Mendonça, J. R. C., & Cassundé, F. R. S. A. (2016a). The interaction between the role of academic manager and managerial competences: Perceptions of teachers from a federal university. *Organizações em Contexto, 12*(23), 287–325.

Barbosa, M. A. C., Mendonça, J. R. C., & Cassundé, F. R. S. A. (2016b). Managerial competences (expected versus perceived) of academic managers of federal higher education institution: Perceptions of teachers from a federal university. *Administração: Ensino e Pesquisa, 17*(3), 439–473. https://doi.org/10.13058/raep.2016.V17n3.344

Barbosa, M. A. C., Paiva, K. C. M., & Mendonça, J. R. C. (2018). Social role and professional and managerial competences of higher education professor: Similarities between the constructs and research perspectives. *Organizações & Sociedade, 25*(84), 100–121. https://doi.org/10.1590/1984-9240846

Bessant, C., & Mavin, S. (2016). Neglected on the front line: Tensions and challenges for the first-line manager-academic role in UK business schools. *Journal of Management Development, 35*(7), 916–929. https://doi.org/10.1108/JMD-09-2014-0105

Braun, V., & Clarke, V. (2014). What can "thematic analysis" offer health and wellbeing researchers? *International Journal of Qualitative Studies on Health and Well-being, 9*(1). https://doi.org/10.3402/qhw.v9.26152

Broadbent, J. (2011). Discourses of control, managing the boundaries. *The British Accounting Review, 43*(4), 264–277. https://doi.org/10.1016/j.bar.2011.08.003

Bruni, A., Gherardi, S., & Parolin, L. L. (2007). Knowing in a system of frag-mented knowledge. *Mind, Culture, and Activity, 14*(1–2), 83–102. https://doi.org/10.1080/10749030701307754

Castro, D., & Tomàs, M. (2011). Development of manager-academics at insti-tutions of higher education in Catalonia. *Higher Education Quarterly, 65*(3), 290–307. https://doi.org/10.1111/j.1468-2273.2011.00490.x

Chia, R. (2017). A process-philosophical understanding of organizational learning as "wayfinding" process, practices and sensitivity to environmental affordances. *The Learning Organization, 24*(2), 107–118. https://doi.org/10.1108/TLO-11-2016-0083

Clegg, S. (2003). *Managing organization futures in a changing world of power/knowledge*. Oxford University Press.

Cuel, R. (2020). A journey of learning organization in social science: Interview with Silvia Gherardi. *Learning Organization, 27*(5), 455–461. https://doi.org/10.1108/TLO-02-2020-0031

Davis, A., Jansen van Rensburg, M., & Venter, P. (2016). The impact of managerialism on the strategy work of university middle managers. *Studies in Higher Education, 41*(8), 1480–1494. https://doi.org/10.1080/03075079.2014.981518

Deem, R., & Brehony, K. J. (2005). Management as ideology: The case of 'new managerialism' in higher education. *Oxford Review of Education, 31*(2), 217–235. https://doi.org/10.1080/03054980500117827

Deem, R., & Johnson, R. (2003). Risking the university? Learning to be a manager-academic in UK universities. *Sociological Research Online, 8*(3), 1–15. https://doi.org/10.5153/sro.819

Dowling-Hetherington, L. (2014). The changing demands of academic life in Ireland. *International Journal of Educational Management, 28*, 141–151. https://doi.org/10.1108/IJEM-02-2013-0021

Durante, D. G., et al. (2019). Organizational learning in practice-based studies approach: Review of scientific production. *Revista de Adminis-tração Mackenzie, 20*(2), 1–27. https://doi.org/10.1590/1678-6971/eRA MG190131

El-Awad, Z., Brattström, A., & Breugst, N. (2022). Bridging cognitive scripts in multidisciplinary academic spinoff teams: A process perspective on how academics learn to work with non-academic managers. *Research Policy, 51*(10). https://doi.org/10.1016/j.respol.2022.104592

Elkjaer, B. (2022). Taking stock of "Organizational Learning": Looking back and moving forward. *Management Learning, 53*(3), 582–604. https://doi.org/10.1177/13505076211049599

Ésther, A. B. (2011). The managerial competencies of the deans of federal universities in Minas Gerais: The perception of top management. *Cadernos*

EBAPE.BR, *9*, 648–667. https://doi.org/10.1590/S1679-395120110006 00011

Frenkel, S. J. (2021). Embedded in two worlds: The university academic manager's work, identity and social relations. *Educational Management Administration & Leadership*, *51*(5), 1–18. https://doi.org/10.1177/174 11432211027643

Geschwind, L., Aarrevaara, T., Berg, L. N., & Lind, J. K. (2019a). The changing roles of academic leaders: Decision-making, power, and performance. In R. Pinheiro, L. Geschwind, H. F. Hansen, & K. Pulkkinen (Eds.), *Reforms, organizational change and performance in higher education: A comparative account from the Nordic countries* (pp. 181–210). Springer Nature. https://doi.org/10.1007/978-3-030-11738-2_6

Geschwind, L., Kekäle, J., Pinheiro, R., & Sørensen, M. P. (2019b). Responsible universities in context. In M. P. Sørensen, L. Geschwind, J. Kekäle, & R. Pinheiro (Eds.), *The responsible university: Exploring the Nordic context and beyond* (pp. 3–29). Springer Nature. https://doi.org/10.1007/978-3-030-25646-3_1

Gherardi, S. (2001). From organizational learning to practice-based knowing. *Human Relations*, *54*(1), 131–139. https://doi.org/10.1177/001872670 1541016

Gherardi, S. (2006). Organizational knowledge: The texture of workplace learning. *Scandinavian Journal of Management*, *23*(2), 223–225. https://doi.org/10.1016/j.scaman.2007.03.001

Gherardi, S. (2008). Situated knowledge and situated action: What do practice-based studies promise? In D. Barry, & H. Hansen (Eds.), *The SAGE handbook of new approaches in management and organization* (pp. 516–527). Sage.

Gherardi, S. (2009). Knowing and learning in practice-based studies: An introduction. *Learning Organization*, *16*(5), 352–359. https://doi.org/10.1108/09696470910974144

Gherardi, S. (2015). Why Kurt Wolff matters for a practice-based perspective of sensible knowledge in ethnography. *Journal of Organizational Ethnography*, *4*(1), 117–131. https://doi.org/10.1108/JOE-11-2013-0021

Gherardi, S. (2019). *How to conduct a practice-based study: Problems and methods*. Edward Elgar Publishing.

Gherardi, S. (2021). A posthumanist epistemology of practice. In C. Neesham (Ed.), *Handbook of philosophy of management, handbooks in philosophy*. Springer. https://doi.org/10.1007/978-3-319-48352-8_53-1

Gherardi, S., & Perrotta, M. (2014). Becoming a practitioner: Professional learning as a social practice. In S. Billett, C. Harteis, & H. Gruber (Eds.), *International handbook of research in professional and practice-based learning* (pp. 139–162). Springer. https://doi.org/10.1007/978-94-017-8902-8_6

Hess, A. (2023). "Last orders, please!": The disappearance of communicative spaces at universities. *Irish Journal of Sociology*, *31*(3), 354–373. https://doi.org/10.1177/07916035231184786

Hopwood, N. (2014). Four essential dimensions of workplace learning. *Journal of Workplace Learning*, 26(6/7), 349–363. https://doi.org/10.1108/JWL-09-2013-0069

Iorga, M. (2011). Being workaholic in the university. Teacher, researcher or manager? *AGATHOS—An International Review of the Humanities and Social Sciences*, 2(2), 129–138.

Johnson, R. (2002). Learning to manage the university: Tales of training and experience. *Higher Education Quarterly*, 56(1), 33–51. https://doi.org/10.1111/1468-2273.00201

Johnson, R. N., & Deem, R. (2003). Talking of students: Tensions and contradictions for the manager-academic and the university in contemporary higher education. *Higher Education*, 46, 289–314.

Jones, G. A., & Weinrib, J. (2022). The changing context of academic work: Fragmentation, institutional horizontal diversity and vertical stratification. In C. S. Sarrico, M. J. Rosa, & T. Carvalho (Eds.), *Research handbook on academic careers and managing academics* (pp. 36–46). Edward Elgar Publishing. https://doi.org/10.4337/9781839102639.00010

Krücken, G., Blümel, A., & Kloke, K. (2013). The managerial turn in higher education? On the interplay of organizational and occupational change in German academia. *Minerva*, 51, 417–442. https://doi.org/10.1007/s11024-013-9240-z

Lee, C. F., & Amjadi, M. (2014). The role of materiality: Knowing through objects in work practice. *European Management Journal*, 32(5), 723–734. https://doi.org/10.1016/j.emj.2014.01.004

Loveday, V. (2021). 'Under attack': Responsibility, crisis and survival anxiety amongst manager-academics in UK universities. *The Sociological Review*, 69(5), 903–919. https://doi.org/10.1177/0038026121999209

Machovcová, K., Zábrodská, K., & Mudrák, J. (2019). Department heads negotiating emerging managerialism: The Central Eastern European context. *Educational Management Administration & Leadership*, 47(5), 712–729. https://doi.org/10.1177/1741143217753193

Martin, Q. (2022). From faculty to administration: Preparing the next generation of academic leaders. *Perspectives: Policy and Practice in Higher Education*, 26(3), 109–114. https://doi.org/10.1080/13603108.2021.2016513

Mattsson, P., Perez Vico, E., & Salö, L. (2023). Introduction: Universities and the matter of mattering. In P. Mattsson, E. P. Vico, & L. Salö (Eds.), *Making universities matter: Collaboration, engagement, impact* (pp. 1–10). Springer Nature. https://doi.org/10.1007/978-3-031-48799-6_1

Mintzberg, H. (2015). Time for the plural sector. *Stanford Social Innovation Review*, 13(3), 28–33.

Nicolini, D. (2012). *Practice theory, work & organization*. Oxford University Press.

Nicolini, D., Gherardi, S., & Yanow, D. (2003). Introduction: Toward a practice-based view of knowing and learning in organizations. In D. Nicolini, S.

Gherardi, & D. Yanow (Eds.), *Knowing in organizations: A practice-based approach* (pp. 3–31). M. E. Sharpe. https://doi.org/10.4324/978131529 0973

Orlikowski, W. J. (2002). Knowing in practice: Enacting a collective capability in distributed organizing. *Organization Science, 13*(3), 249–273. https://doi. org/10.1287/orsc.13.3.249.2776

Orlikowski, W. J., & Scott, S. V. (2015). Exploring material-discursive practices. *Journal of Management Studies, 52*(5), 697–705. https://doi.org/10.1111/ joms.12114

Price, O. M., Gherardi, S., & Manidis, M. (2020). Enacting responsible management: A practice-based perspective. In O. Laasch, et al. (Eds.), *Research handbook of responsible management* (pp. 392–409). Edward Elgar Publishing. https://doi.org/10.4337/9781788971966.00035

Protasio, M., & Tauchen, G. (2021). The academic manager in the coordination of undergraduate courses: An integrative review. *Poíesis Pedagógica, 19.* https://doi.org/10.5216/rppoi.v19.70779

Rodrigues, A. C. A. L., & Villardi, B. Q. (2017). Teacher training for university management: An inductive analysis of the professors of the stricto sensu postgraduation from UFRRJ. *Revista Foco, 10*(2), 208–231. https://doi.org/10. 28950/1981-223x_revistafocoadm/2017.v10i2.408

Scaratti, G., Gorli, M., & Ripamonti, S. (2009). The power of professionally situated practice analysis in redesigning organizations. *Journal of Workplace Learning, 21*(7), 538–554. https://doi.org/10.1108/13665620910985531

Silva, E. R., & Larentis, F. (2022). Storytelling from experience to reflection: ERSML cycle of organizational learning. *The International Journal of Human Resource Management, 33*(4), 686–709. https://doi.org/10.1080/ 09585192.2020.1737831

Silva, F. M. V. (2012). The transition to university management: The meaning of interpersonal relationships. *Revista de Administração FACES Journal, 11*(4), 72–91.

Silva, F. M. V., & Cunha, C. J. C. (2015). Be leaving university manager: The interpesonal relationship. *Diálogo e Interação, 9*(1). https://doi.org/10. 1590/1980-265X-TCE-2019-0057

Winter, R. (2009). Academic manager or managed academic? Academic identity schisms in higher education. *Journal of Higher Education Policy and Management, 31*(2), 121–131. https://doi.org/10.1080/13600800902825835

Winter, R. P. (2017). Managing academics. In *Managing academics: A question of perspective* (pp. 7–18). Edward Elgar Publishing. https://doi.org/10.4337/ 9781781006696.00007

The Cauldron of Knowing of the Academic Manager

Abstract Knowing-in-practice notion highlights the role of human action in organizational work in situated contexts, in which knowing is a social condition for learning a practice. Due to its complex nature, university management and the role of the academic manager are suitable fields to consider this theoretical focus, as our research findings have evidenced. Involving the knowing-in-practice notion and the academic manager in the study has resulted in the proposition of a framework, named The Cauldron of Knowing of the Academic Manager. In this chapter, we briefly develop the elements that are part of this framework. We deepen the culinary metaphor regarding the academic manager's knowing, the way the framework's elements are connected, and the dynamic behind these connections. Some implications for university management are presented.

Keywords Knowing-in-practice · University management · Academic manager · Academic manager's knowing

Our research has enabled the definition of 9 analytical categories, based on the 43 microcategories that emerged from the findings: (a) connecting to management, (b) maturing as a manager, (c) disconnecting from management, (d) dealing with structure and processes, (e) dealing with oneself, (f) dealing with the nature of the academic and manager relationship, (g) dealing with power, (h) dealing with external connections, and (i) dealing with internal connections. These analytical categories together have led us to the proposition of a framework, called "The Cauldron of Knowing of the Academic Manager" (Fig. 2.1).

In this chapter, we briefly conceptualize each of the analytical categories and explain the constituting parts of the framework, including the reasons to contemplate a culinary metaphor. We only list the microcategories related to each analytical category. In the next chapters we deepen their definitions and features.

The framework has been designed with an emphasis on a processual logic, in which the elements interact and depend on one another. This is the reason why we have adopted a culinary metaphor, in which the elements that make up knowing are part of food in a broth, in a clay cauldron. This material for the cauldron has been chosen due to the chemical interactions and the cooking time that preserve the nutritional value in a peculiar way. Regarding such aspects, we highlight knowing being configured from and with culture, language, labor divisions, and power relations (Antonello & Godoy, 2010).

In the center of the cauldron one can find the analytical categories (food in the broth) "Connecting to management", "Maturing as a manager", and "Disconnecting from management". As represented by the ellipses, the categories interact through the spaces of intersection. The dashed lines aim to reinforce the interactions between these categories and with the broth, in order to preserve the processual notion adopted in the study.

These categories are directly associated to the academic manager's path. Connecting to management is related to the professor's paths and experiences before performing a role as academic manager, as well as the first moments in university management. Professors can have different levels of involvement before joining university management. Maturing as a manager encompasses the way professors become academic managers, as they develop and deepen their roles as managers. Disconnecting from management is related to the process, moment, and context in which academic managers withdraw from management activities. It is important to stress that the academic manager's path is constituted in time and space and does not necessarily follow a linearity, which means a context in which it is situated. The correspondent microcategories are presented in Table 2.1.

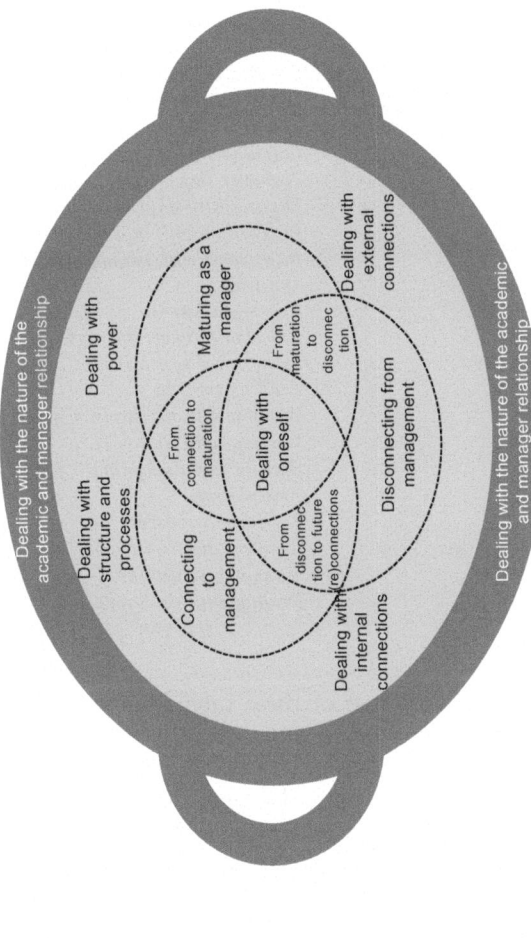

Fig. 2.1   Framework: The cauldron of knowing of the academic manager

Table 2.1 From connecting to management to disconnecting from management (food)

Analytical category	Microcategory
I. Connecting to management	Connections before management
	Previous knowledge and experience
	Interest in management
	Memories of past actions
	Connections with management
II. Maturing as a manager	Learning from amplitude
	Learning through mistakes
	Learning through pain
	Learning through problem solving
	Dealing with data and their formats
	Interacting with information systems
	Interacting with management methodologies and tools
	Role of documents
	Knowing through reflection
	Memories of past actions
	Reading contexts
	Working with the diversity of activities
	Working with time
	Sharing and dialoguing
	Articulating
	Becoming a reference
III. Disconnecting from management	Concerns about succession
	Managing to detach
	Dealing with the return to teaching

The intersections between two of these categories are called Transition Zones: (a) From connection to maturation, where the elements of connection interact with the beginning of the academic manager's maturation process; (b) From maturation to disconnection, where the elements of maturation combine with the characteristics of disconnection; (c) From disconnection to future (re)connections, where disconnection may serve as a basis and reference for new connections or even reconnections. Such zones are associated with the process of repetition and provisional stabilization and institutionalization of knowing, in which practices represent points of passage for new practices (Bjørkeng et al., 2009; Bruni et al., 2007). These elements are explored in Chapter 3.

Table 2.2 Dealing with oneself (food—central intersection)

Analytical category	Microcategory
Dealing with oneself	Dealing with humility and susceptibilities Dealing with emotions Role of the family

At the framework's central intersection, we indicate the analytical category "Dealing with oneself". This category has been chosen to be in this position due to its general condition of connection to other categories, regarding the academic manager's trajectory, responsibilities, relationships, articulations, emotions, and achievements. In Chapter 3, we present more details about it. This category is associated with the individual and identity elements of the academic manager. Therefore, it can be considered a category that enhances the balance that academic managers seek when dealing with their activities, roles, relationships, and practices. The related microcategories are presented in Table 2.2.

In the broth, in chemical transformation with food, we have the analytical categories called Contextualizing Elements: "Dealing with structure and processes", "Dealing with power", "Dealing with external connections", and "Dealing with internal connections". When we consider the process of becoming an academic manager, which starts from the connection and addresses the disconnection with management, there are actions, decisions, practices, and circumstances associated and connected with the contextualizing elements. Chapter 4 is intended to develop such aspects.

Dealing with structure and processes is associated to hierarchical structures, bureaucracy levels, and the processes encompassing administrative routines, decision taking, and communication. Dealing with power involves aspects that support and connect to the constitution of the condition and capability to influence and direct actions, behaviors, and interests. Dealing with external connections takes into account the features and amplitude level of contacts between the university and its stakeholders. Dealing with internal connections covers the relationship within the university, between the academic managers and their teams, the managers who do not have academic roles and other university structures. The corresponding microcategories are presented in Table 2.3.

The clay cauldron is represented by the analytical category "Dealing with the nature of the academic and manager relationship". This is the

Table 2.3   Contextualizing elements (broth)

Analytical category	Microcategory
I—Dealing with structure and processes	Dealing with hierarchy
	Dealing with processes
II—Dealing with power	Dealing with the authority of the position
	Meanings arising from physical spaces
	Dealing with the contradictory and conflicts
	Dealing with the level of exposure
III—Dealing with external connections	Amplitude and quality of external contacts
	Dealing with students, graduates, and the regional community
	Dealing with organizations outside the region
IV—Dealing with internal connections	Relating to the teams
	Dealing with non-academic managers
	Dealing with support sectors

Table 2.4   Dealing with the nature of the academic and manager relationship (Clay Claundron)

Dealing with the nature of the academic and manager relationship	Teaching contributing to management
	Management contributing to teaching
	Researcher contributing to management
	Weight of the interaction between manager and professor

element that gives and allows a special flavor, since its features are related to the interaction and contributions between the roles and practices as professor/researcher and the roles and practices as manager. In Chapter 5, we explore this category (Table 2.4).

Thus, in a culinary metaphor, the moments of connection, maturation, and disconnection and their intersections, similarly to food, and the contextualizing elements, similarly to the broth, cook in a cauldron, whose clay epitomizes the nature of the professor and manager relationship. Knowing is configured from the academic managers' accomplishments, as they connect to management, mature as managers, and disconnect from management. These moments interact with each other in their transition zones. On the other hand, every one of these moments and zones interacts with the other elements identified in the research, such as dealing with oneself, which plays a central role, and the contextualizing elements, in which aspects associated to power, processes, structures, and relationships are emphasized. Considered together, both the moments and the elements indicated are linked to what we have called "dealing with the nature of the academic and manager relationship".

The knowing-in-practice notion is therefore put into perspective, since we contemplate the role of human action in university situated contexts, in which their social structures are both the production and context of human activities, and knowing transcends the generation and transmission of knowledge (Bruni et al., 2007; Gherardi, 2009; Orlikowski, 2002; Scaratti et al., 2009). Knowing-in-practice can thus be regarded as something social, procedural, cultural, situated, historically and materially mediated, emergent, open, and temporary (Lee & Amjadi, 2014; Nicolini, 2003).

We elaborate this chapter in order to mention the framework's general aspects. Our purpose is to offer readers an integrated perspective before deepening each element. This framework enables researchers and practitioners both a deeper and wider perspective on the circumstances, specificities, dynamics, and contexts related to university management, mainly because we highlight the entanglements and connections that are part of the academic manager's role and knowing. It is important to keep in mind this feature when we interpret and reflect about the framework, since entanglements and connections are about the ontology and character of the knowing-in-practice notion and the academic manager's knowing.

REFERENCES

Antonello, C. S., & Godoy, A. S. (2010). The crossroads of organizational learning: A multiparadigmatic view. *Revista de Administração Contemporânea, 14*, 310–332. https://doi.org/10.1590/S1415-65552010000200008

Bjørkeng, K., Clegg, S., & Pitsis, T. (2009). Becoming (a) practice. *Management Learning, 40*(2), 145–159. https://doi.org/10.1177/1350507608101226

Bruni, A., Gherardi, S., & Parolin, L. L. (2007). Knowing in a system of fragmented knowledge. *Mind, Culture, and Activity, 14*(1–2), 83–102. https://doi.org/10.1080/10749030701307754

Gherardi, S. (2009). Knowing and learning in practice-based studies: An introduction. *Learning Organization, 16*(5), 352–359. https://doi.org/10.1108/09696470910974144

Lee, C. F., & Amjadi, M. (2014). The role of materiality: Knowing through objects in work practice. *European Management Journal, 32*(5), 723–734. https://doi.org/10.1016/j.emj.2014.01.004

Nicolini, D. (2003). *Knowing in organizations: A practice-based approach.* Routledge. https://doi.org/10.4324/9781315290973

Orlikowski, W. J. (2002). Knowing in practice: Enacting a collective capability in distributed organizing. *Organization Science, 13*(3), 249–273. https://doi.org/10.1287/orsc.13.3.249.2776

Scaratti, G., Gorli, M., & Ripamonti, S. (2009). The power of professionally situated practice analysis in redesigning organizations. *Journal of Workplace Learning, 21*(7), 538–554. https://doi.org/10.1108/13665620910985531

Academic Manager's Path: From Connections to Disconnections

Abstract We explore and deepen in this chapter the following elements of the cauldron presented in Chapter 2: Connecting to management; Maturing as a manager; Disconnecting from management; Transition Zones; and Dealing with oneself. These parts are in the center of the cauldron. We present the research findings and some managerial implications for aspects such as previous experiences, connections before management, learning through pain and mistakes, interacting with information systems and management methodologies, knowing through reflection, sharing and dialoguing, dealing with time, dealing with humility and with emotions, concerns about succession, managing to detach, and dealing with the return to teaching.

Keywords Academic manager · Academic manager's path · Academic manager's knowing

This chapter is focused on the academic manager's path, from management connection to management disconnection. It shows how the trajectory of the academic manager is constituted in terms of a contextual and situated aspect, not only in temporal terms, but also in spatial terms—the space and time that the academic manager occupies. We explore the microcategories related to each analytical category, mentioned in

Chapter 2, regarding what we called "Food" in the cauldron: Connecting to management; Maturing as a manager; Disconnecting from management; Transition Zones; and Dealing with oneself. We emphasize that these elements are also connected to the other facets of the cauldron, which will be deepened in the next chapters.

3.1   Connecting to Management

The first analytical category we develop is Connecting to management. As commented in Chapter 2, this category encompasses the professor's trajectory and experiences before entering management. We also consider the first moments and movements in university management. This analytical category consists of the following microcategories: Connections before management; Previous knowledge and experience; Interest in management; Memories of past actions; and Connections with management.

Connections before management involves elements that enable a professor, to some degree, to connect with their future position in university management. The findings show that the invitation to the position is, to some extent, the result of circumstances, such as places, times, roles, and interpersonal interactions formed over time. These interactions comprehended connections with people who were, at some point, involved in management and were considered as references, as well as the approximation developed due to similar worldviews and thinking. We also highlight the initiatives developed as a professor, in the classroom and in other activities linked to education and research, which allowed them to become known to management, however not necessarily prepared for this.

These aspects reinforce the role of interpersonal relationships, which may even induce the acceptance of the invitation to become a manager. As commented by a retired academic manager, someone gets to know the institution, its culture, its concerns, its virtues, its history, and the people within it. According to a statement by a rectory's member, even though the professors' positionings sometimes differed, she always looks for a relationship of dialog with managers, colleagues, and the teams.

Previous knowledge and experience initially embraces learning from management education, such as undergraduate and graduate courses, as well as reading and training related to courses with specific themes, not necessarily linked to management. However, there were reports mentioning lack of prior formal preparation, despite previous connections, lack of initiatives and institutional resources, and the implications for their constitution as university managers. This microcategory also includes the learning difficulties related to management over time and the repercussions on university operations. Therefore, it refers to aspects of the quality of previous qualifications.

Another aspect is associated with the knowledge acquired from the professor's previous experiences, not necessarily in teaching, which contributed to their identification as a potential candidate to become involved in university management. In this context, it is worth mentioning previous preparation to take on a management position, at a certain point in the academic manager's career.

A former academic manager said that she became a manager by practice and ended up taking a course about university management and leadership when she was already in management. Had the course occurred earlier, she would have made fewer mistakes. A coordinator alerts about the disappointment in relation to some professors that present potential to become managers, mainly because they are nice people and good professors.

Associated with previous knowledge and experiences, Memories of past actions involves management experiences and initiatives in the institution's history, which are not necessarily documented. These elements, as emphasized by some interviewees in the research (undergraduate and graduate coordinators), are necessary to understand the institutional mission throughout its history and to avoid repeating past mistakes. In this respect, as new administrations took office, there were situations of unrecovered records, whether intentionally or not. It is worth mentioning situations where management actions reappeared under different names, without being clear whether past records and experiences were taken into account. A retired academic manager mentioned the deliberate attempts to disregard determined past actions and initiatives in former rectory's mandates, which have been resumed recently.

Interest in management is associated with previous knowledge and connections prior to management. This interest also contemplates situations in which initially there was no interest in management, but this aspect changed as contact was made with those who were already academic managers. As commented by a campus director, she never really thought about being a manager, but it just happened, things progressed. A coordinator highlighted that she as a professor was always looking for something, a desire to move up, a restlessness to do different things, to be challenged.

Connections with management encompasses the moments, processes, and circumstances in which the professor's first contacts and interactions as a manager take place. Situations emerged associated firstly with the welcoming of the new manager by staff, academic managers, and non-academic managers, the process regarding the level of openness, the quality of the welcome, and the attitude toward the learning process (apprentice spirit) of both those who welcome and those who are welcomed.

Secondly, we have identified situations that require dealing with new friends and interested stakeholders that arise with management. It includes other newcomers to management when there is, for example, a change in management at the rectory, as well as those who want to connect or stay connected to management. Another point is the time it takes to comprehend and appropriate operational management issues, such as bureaucratic activities and rites, in which employees play a critical role. This aspect also depends on the new manager's openness to learning and their ability to relate to people at different hierarchical levels.

As mentioned by a coordinator, when someone takes up a position, there will be new friends and sharing of ideas, but also some resistance. An employee commented that there were several talks with new academic managers when she explained the activities, in order to get them situated about the features of the job. From there they work together, although some professors may be less patient to listen and learn.

3.2   Maturing as a Manager

Maturing as a manager covers the way professors become academic managers, taking into account the development and deepening of their roles as managers. There are several challenges associated to the complexity of this process, such as in problem solving, decision taking, and in interpersonal relationships, with regard to the diversity of personal characteristics, conditions, and contexts to mature, including sociomaterial aspects. It is also important to note that these aspects were built predominantly through informal learning. This analytical category consists of the following microcategories: learning from amplitude, through mistakes, through pain, and through problem solving; knowing through reflection, memories of past actions, and reading contexts;

working with the diversity of activities, and with time; sharing and dialoguing, articulating, and becoming a reference; role of documents, dealing with data and their formats, interacting with information systems, and with management methodologies and tools.

Learning from amplitude encompasses elements associated with the ability to recognize, consider, and appropriate different perspectives and points of view. The findings show situations in which different possibilities and insights were explored and inserted into what the academic manager considered to be previous truths, therefore linking them to a short- and long-term vision when making decisions and solving problems within the context of routine management. In this respect, an interviewee commented on the relationship between a broad and a narrow mindset. A broad mindset could be seen by him as a way to improve the academic manager's "radar". A rectory's member refers to it as a contemplative attitude, which takes a continuous look at the timeline, seeing the parts and the whole and vice-versa. According to a retired academic manager, when people are listened to, they can let go of prejudices and ingrained ideas. They listen and then everyone can work together, but first it is necessary to be humble enough to listen to them.

Learning through mistakes arises from the academic manager's practices, when they consider their own mistakes and others', including preconceived ideas and ideological aspects. In the meantime, there are situations of admitting and recognizing, or not, the results of past decisions, such as when there was a mistake in choosing a certain person for a position, as well as the importance of dialogue and consideration of criteria in order to make fewer mistakes in the future.

As a rectory's member mentioned, there is the constitution of the manager as they move forward, with their mistakes, pains, and achievements. Another rectory's member emphasized, although someone may master something from a conceptual point of view, and they want to master it in practice, there is no superpower to know everything, including knowing how to do things and also knowing how to know.

In Learning through pain, questions arose about learning from the difficulties caused by the university structure and challenging decision-making, such as having to dismiss a fellow professor, often a friend. In other words, situations that cause discomfort and pain in management. This includes suffering in certain processes of change, both individually and collectively. Moreover, one has to deal with those who do not believe that changes will take place in a new administration and who are ready to voice their opinions, the so-called "ominous birds" according to a knowledge area's director. On the other hand, another knowledge area's director commented on his difficulty to fire a professor because it is a source of anxiety and stress, even though the process is carried out by a collegiate body.

In the microcategory Learning through problem solving, we have identified the possibility for academic managers to come into contact with different ways of dealing with problems, to learn to deal with justice in decisions, to deal with conflicts arising from the quest to solve problems and the existence of dialogue as a source of resolution. There was also the pleasure of seeing a certain project implemented after various conflicts and clashes, or as an interviewee put it (rectory), from the field of problems to the field of solutions. In this context, a knowledge area's director recognizes the role of the manager as being in charge of solving problems while leveraging people's potential. A coordinator talked about some people that try to stay away from him, due to some situations he had to rush a bit to solve. Although the person was unable or unwilling to solve the situation, the solution was found.

The findings related to Knowing through reflection address situations in which reflection is presented and constituted, such as learning through and with criticism and significant moments that allow insights. These moments also occurred in short-term qualification courses, such as the institution's Management Development Program, and long-term courses, such as the MBA in University Management. Both elements depend on the quality and condition of the reflection, stemming from the situations, circumstances, and contexts presented, associated with the attitude of how one reflects.

As a rectory's member explored, people have to digest criticisms, it is about how someone absorbs criticisms and the points made by others, which can be distorted. In this case, the criticism, which was supposed to be constructive, is not internalized. In this case, a coordinator remembered a meeting in which she was severely criticized, due to her lack of the context understanding at that moment. It was a moment of great reflection and marked her trajectory in management. As she mentioned, it was as if the one who criticized her took her by the shoulders and told her: calm down, understand what you are getting into, take ownership of this context, and situate yourself.

Memories of past actions, when considering the maturation process of the academic manager, is associated with the level of interest and appropriation of what was done by individuals in the past, including situations of forgetting, even if deliberately. In the meantime, a rectory's member brought up Paulo Freire's concept of historicity: what we have today is the fruit of accumulated experience and many have contributed to it, so it is offensive and disrespectful to disregard the actions and initiatives from those who came before us. A coordinator exemplifies a change of management in the past marked by going backward, a way of managing marked by going backward.

Reading contexts is related to the understanding and interpretation of contexts that surround the academic manager. According to the findings, it involves sensing the atmosphere of the environment, learning from the warnings and signs, whether weak or strong, knowing how to contextualize and being able to interpret coincidences, as well as seeing further ahead, with an approach that can be called more strategic. As indicated by a rectory's member, to carry out a "hermeneutic reading", in other words, to understand what is happening based on the trajectory and reality of those involved. According to him, the reality does not come purely to us, we always understand and interpret it. And then there is our education, and if we have a broader education, we can understand and filter data and information in a much more assertive way. In this context, a former academic manager and now retired mentioned that all the experiences that are opening up perspectives are going to open up new horizons.

Working with the diversity of activities is associated with the variety of interactions, approaches, and attitudes with which the academic manager interacts with both superiors and subordinates, including non-professors and fellow professors, as well as people from outside the university. As stated by a coordinator, sometimes "we stumble on our activities". In this regard, a campus director commented on the importance of knowing how to navigate between management and teaching activities and roles.

In this case, a knowledge's area director alerted that the day-to-day activities of the manager are very absorbing and they break up the routine too much, specifically when he should prioritize activities that demand more concentration, such as the data analysis in a research or a class's content organization. This situation taught him to deal with the schedule in a different way. The good aspect is that every day the academic manager has something new.

Working with time covers the exercise of choosing priorities, organizing activities and perceiving the temporality of those involved (dealing with different timings), given the myriad of roles and activities with which the academic manager is involved and committed. This creates a work rhythm that relates to the rhythm of other people, including subordinate teams, superiors, the rest of the academic community, and people outside the university. As mentioned by a coordinator, there is a need to give it time to mature, because there are different rhythms. In this sense, a coordinator and a knowledge area's director draw attention to the time dedicated to management, which can lead to dumbing down of other capabilities, including when the academic manager is unable to enjoy and learn from the time spent.

Sharing and dialoguing involves the continuous development of the ability to listen, consider, and be open to the ideas of various audiences through conversations. Moreover, this microcategory comprehends the way in which academic managers position themselves and elaborate their arguments, including situations in order to be heard by others later, showing a certain willingness to deal with conflicts, which may or may not have a constructive bias. From the sharing and interactions with people at different levels of knowledge and experience, including institutionalized collegiate decision-making spaces, despite a lack of organized moments for this purpose, it takes into account the participation of a certain number of people in the management process. Although this may not have been the intention from the start, there is also learning to put oneself in the other people's shoes, in other words, the exercise of empathy.

A campus director highlights the importance of being "a sounding box" for different publics, such as students and professors. According to a former manager, it is also important to manage from the hallways by leaving the office. In such aspects, a knowledge area's director states that it does not matter if someone is a manager or a professor, instead what matters is the position in which they are. According to him, academic managers are conflict mediators, putting themselves in other people's shoes, understanding what they are bringing, understanding the pain, and the conflicts needed to be mediated.

Articulating is associated with the way in which the academic manager interacts, organizes, and gets involved in terms of political actions and influence in their area of activity, in the context of the power forces present. This microcategory is also associated with the analytical category "Dealing with power". In the findings, we have identified aspects such as knowing how to observe the relationship of power forces between the actors involved, learning from the opportunities that come with the position (authority), playing the political game, and knowing how to represent by lending their voice to the university. We also highlight the concerns of being aware of the distance between discourses and practices, as well as the ability to circulate in different spaces, both internal and external to the university.

As emphasized by a coordinator, the importance to take time to observe the context, the players, and the power relations between them. These aspects are related to another coordinator's comment, in which academic managers have to realize that they do not do anything alone, they make decisions together with their peers, they do not pick a fight alone, the higher one's intellectual level of people, the greater the analysis and the greater the empowerment they have.

Becoming a reference is the way in which academic managers legitimize themselves to the public with which they are involved, to the extent that, in their articulations, attitudes, actions, and results, they gain respect and trust as managers through their actions and relationships, realizing that they are recognized by their peers. In other words, there is legitimacy in practice, to the point in which those who were looking for a reference are now considered a reference, even after professors leave management. On the other hand, there comes a time when being a reference in one area becomes a barrier to other activities.

A knowledge area's director, talking about his path at university, commented that he worked for a while with an extremely experienced professor, who had been a former director. He had his doctor's degree when he got involved in management, but he was 32 years old, as a consequence there was the question of affirmation in the eyes of colleagues, peers, a delicate issue within academia. Having the qualifications is different from being recognized as a leader by the peers. On the other hand, as a way to perceive an academic manager becoming a reference, an employee reinforced the moment that a new coordinator started to have more contact with professors, to be more in demand by the professors, with issues being solved without the employee's help.

These elements also take us to consider the role of sociomaterial aspects as maturing as a manager. From the findings related to hierarchy, methodologies, physical spaces, systems, data formats, and documents, we take into account the work practices performed by humans and non-humans, due to the complex network between people, activities, ideas, information, and material artifacts (Bruni et al., 2007; Gherardi, 2009, 2019; Orlikowski & Scott, 2015).

Dealing with data and their formats involves the way in which the academic manager learns to access and understand data, mainly quantitative, in a context of achieving results and generating targets, therefore transforming it into certain information and leading to certain levels of generalization, as well as understanding and creating indicators. Another aspect is associated with the way in which the academic manager chooses and presents certain information over others, including graphical aspects. We also have identified the moments of defending and negotiating their decisions, actions, and teams from information with a determined quality, accuracy, and impact, as commented by a coordinator.

Interacting with information systems is associated with the way in which the academic manager establishes connections with the structures of the information systems, which are directly related to the structuring of internal operational processes and flows. The interviewees mentioned how the university's information systems for consultation, approvals, analysis, and decision-making interfere with the consumption of the individual's time, which does not happen only during working hours, but also when they are called away on an emergency or need to use their time away from work to prepare analyses and proposals, as mentioned by a knowledge area's director. We also have identified the information itself and its format serving as an instrument of control, which can be identified as the non-human consuming and controlling the human.

In this regard, another aspect that emerged was what one interviewee called the oppression of systems. At the same time, situations were mentioned such as the use of e-mail in copy as a form of pressure for certain people and the agenda that commands people's lives, depending on how it is used. An example is Google Calendar being filled in whenever there are spaces as if the academic manager were free in all of them, as emphasized by a rectory's member.

In Interacting with management methodologies and tools, we address points associated with the calculation and presentation of targets that reinforce, minimize, and hide the differences between areas of knowledge and campuses; management tools that highlight certain academic managers to the detriment of others, depending on the circumstances and articulations; the way in which the criteria for elaborating, monitoring and evaluating plans and projects of the areas are established and negotiated; the way in which operational flows are established, such as the system of professor occupation and the movement it generates in the composition of professor's working hours. In addition, the findings have revealed the coexistence of management tools from the past and the present, even if those from the past are only in the memory of the older academic managers and staff, as well as the academic managers and non-academic managers who are deluded by the numbers, associated with the urgency of making certain decisions, as a coordinator commented.

Role of documents concerns the way in which academic managers deal with the intricacies and interpretations of external legislation in its various formats, especially those associated with Education and Innovation, as well as the internal resolutions and instructions established, including draft formats and structures for projects and plans. In this sense, due to the university's need to ensure its sustainability and presence in the community, the interviewees highlighted multiple times dealing with contracts, agreements, and terms of cooperation and how they learn from participating in their drafting, which may involve people outside the institution, with words and expressions permitted and avoided. Another aspect is the level of contact and appropriation of highly relevant university documents, given that they are collective creations, such as strategic and institutional plans, as a coordinator highlighted, due to the university management peculiarities.

3.3 Disconnecting from Management

As previously presented, Disconnecting from management is associated to the moment, process, and context in which academic managers withdraw from management activities. This analytical category is represented by three microcategories: concerns about succession, managing to detach, and dealing with the return to teaching.

Concerns about succession relates to expectations of the effects of the professors leaving management, both on themselves and others, and what disempowerment will mean, both in operational, relational, and emotional terms, taking into account the legacy that remains and how much it is taken into account. The transition does not only happen with those who leave, but also with those who remain, and there may be a reciprocal climate of anguish.

An employee commented that she felt anguish about her vice-chancellor in moments of change in rectory, because at some point he would no longer be her leader and the work would not be continued. In this context, a rectory's member mentioned his concerns about leaving management, that it is not permanent. He loves teaching, he would feel very uncomfortable not working in teaching anymore. However, during the period in management, he was away from teaching undergraduate courses and he got tense thinking about it, that he would be back.

In Managing to detach, the academic manager seeks and creates the conditions for leaving management and returning only to teaching or even to lower hierarchical levels of management, even with the possibility of resistance. For example, a rectory's member or director becomes the coordinator of an undergraduate course or graduate program. When returning to teaching without any further management activities, an important element identified has been the ability to distance oneself from certain people, to resume relationships with certain colleagues, and develop new relationships and how painful this process was. In other words, a process of reconnecting to teaching and research, with resulting feelings that can be positive or negative due to the change in the nature of ties.

These aspects are associated with changes in prioritization and positioning, based on their experiences and trajectory in management, to the point where some realized that they had left management, but management had not left them. People leaving management may affect those who remain in management, including situations of discontinuity.

According to a rectory's member, maturity also allows us to make choices, to distance ourselves from what we are experiencing, to have the discernment and to also have the maturity to say no to some things as well as to redefine our own life path in a vibration on a different frequency. On the other hand, an employee talked about the moment when a certain academic manager left management. The employee perceived that the academic manager was relieved for leaving management, but he felt a bit left out by the distance between him and the other managers, due to his interest to keep contributing to university management. Another employee commented that apparently with each new manager the team has to remodel and learn how to follow that person: it is the same job, but it is not the same way.

Dealing with the return to teaching involves the challenges faced by professors who cease to be managers when they need to reconnect with teaching and research, leaving a circuit of which they were a part. There are other attributions and involvement with activities and people when they were academic managers or only professors, which even interferes with the assignment of teaching hours.

In this sense, one former manager commented that she felt like an intruder when he returned to teaching. According to her, there is a loss when leaving management, she came back as professor, had to be re-engaged in research projects, as if she was starting a new career, not in the same place where she had started as a professor. On the other hand, a retired professor and former rector mentioned that if he had ended his university career in this management position, he would have been very frustrated. Returning to the classroom was wonderful for him because he had time to listen, to see, to have contact with peers and students, to talk to students, to listen to them, to work with them, to see them grow, and growing along with them as well.

3.4   Transition Zones

We propose three Transition Zones, called "From connection to maturation", "From maturation to disconnection", and "From disconnection to future (re)connections". These zones are related to the intersections we have in the center of the cauldron, between the categories associated to the academic manager's path. They represent the process of repetition, provisional stabilization, and institutionalization of knowing, in which practices can be considered as points of passage for new practices (Bjørkeng et al., 2009; Bruni et al., 2007).

In the Transition Zone nominated "From connection to maturation", the elements that are part of connecting to management interact with the elements pertaining to the category "maturing as a manager". Aspects such as connections before management, former experiences and knowledge, past actions and their memory, interest in management, and the academic manager's first connections with management interact with the features related to the academic manager's development process.

In other words, the first moments and background an academic manager embraces and configures interconnect with this development. They depend on the dynamic of learning and knowing in terms of contexts and amplitude, diversity of activities, time and past actions, mistakes, reflection, pain, sharing, articulating, problem solving, and the emergence of references. We also have the sociomaterial elements, such as documents, systems, methodologies, and tools. Therefore, we can perceive academic managers' knowing in flux, dependent on both temporal and spatial context, and power and sociomaterial facets (Bjørkeng et al., 2009; Gherardi, 2019; Johnson, 2002; Lee & Amjadi, 2014; Loveday, 2021; Martin, 2022; Nicolini, 2003; Orlikowski & Scott, 2015; Winter, 2009). We reinforce the importance of the first connections the academic manager develops on the quality and diversity of the maturation process.

When we contemplate the Transition Zone "From maturation to disconnection", the features associated to the academic manager development, previously mentioned, interacts with succession reflections and apprehensions, as well as the movements and actions to detach and then return to teaching. The amplitude, quality, and strength of work configured by an academic manager during the management path is assessed, challenged, and constrained when the disconnection from management appears on the horizon, which includes situations where the trustworthiness and reasonability of decisions are questioned.

This disconnection affects both academic managers and other individuals that stablish relationships with them, mostly the teams, the managers who remain, and the professors. The professor that entered management is different compared to the one that leaves management, both to oneself and to others. There is a need to recover some spaces, not only to update and upgrade some skills.

From disconnection to future (re)connections, the last Transition Zone, takes into account that the academic manager's path can suggest a circular feature. Some academic managers can return to management after a period acting only as professor/researcher, in which the disconnections may serve as a basis and reference for new connections in management, embracing different management roles or hierarchical levels, as well as reconnections into former positions.

These situations depend not only on technical conditions or expertise to take office, but also on power issues, due to certain political movements and interpersonal relationships with the university management (Bjørkeng et al., 2009; Gherardi, 2019; Johnson, 2002; Loveday, 2021; Martin, 2022; Orlikowski & Scott, 2015; Winter, 2009). In this case, the culinary metaphor becomes clear, due to the entanglements between the food (academic manager's path) and the cauldron's broth: issues related to structure, power, and internal and external connections (contextualizing elements), aspects that we elaborate in the next chapter.

3.5   Dealing with Oneself

Inserted in the central intersection of the cauldron, this analytical category is associated with the individual and identity elements of the academic manager, which aim to find a balance that academic managers seek due to their roles, relationships, and practices. It is made up of the microcategories "Dealing with humility and susceptibilities"; "Dealing with emotions"; "Role of the family". As commented in Chapter 2, we consider this category the one that assumes a general condition of connection to the other categories previously explored and deepened, including the transition zones. We also emphasize with this category the way academic managers build their trajectories and the role of their responsibilities, emotions, articulations, achievements, relationships, knowing, and practices.

Dealing with humility and susceptibilities is associated with academic managers being willing to ask others for help and acknowledging how much they do not know about a given situation or problem, despite their deep and specialized knowledge in other areas pertaining to the nature of being a professor or researcher. It also involves dealing with other people's levels of humility, as well as how one relates to one's own ego and other's ego. According to a coordinator, it is about sharing things, not just in the sense of delegating, but also sharing the anguish, sharing the need for help, because there are managers who suffer a lot from not being able to ask for help. A rectory's member alerts about the peacock stereotype, the people that always want to be in evidence. There comes a time when they have to finish it, they are going to turn into little birds.

Dealing with emotions pertains the ways in which academic managers vent their tensions and control them, as well as how they react to their feelings, in situations that were considered positive, such as achieving a desired result, or negative, at times when they felt humiliated, hurt or indignant, or ambiguous, such as the role of anxiety. In this context, some interviewees mentioned humor as a necessary element in the academic manager's routine. The "mirror metaphor" was also mentioned by a rectory's member, taking into account how the emotions of certain people have an effect on others and vice-versa. As commented by a coordinator, management has several stressful moments, especially with the overlapping of activities and commitments, which make her anxious.

Role of the family is considered both an element of comfort and support for the exercise of management and tension due to the lack of attention and time that the academic manager would like to provide. On the other hand, from a perspective of trajectory and past, the importance of previous both family support and teachings that have contributed to the current role of academic manager, as indicated by a campus director. According to her, the need to be recognized, to make a difference, and to do a good job, is not just a question of maturity or development, it is also associated to previous family guidelines, support, and teaching.

3.6   Discussion and Implications

The path through which academic managers configure their knowing is complex and multifaceted, since they are supposed to handle the dynamics and the challenging issues of university management, while maintaining the connections with teaching and research. We highlight knowing as a collective activity situated in work practices, in the fragmented, distributed, and dynamic university management landscape (Gherardi & Miele, 2018; Rodrigues & Villardi, 2017).

Professors can have different levels of interest, experiences, and involvement before joining university management. When maturing as managers, a process which encompasses the way they become academic managers, they develop and deepen their roles as managers and at the same time deal with the keeping of their identity as professors. Disconnecting from management is related to the process, moment, and context in which academic managers withdraw from management activities, embracing a diversity of directions from decision taking, emotions with several scopes and intensities, and changes with relationships, including the resuming of old friendships.

However, this process can present a circular logic, in which professors can become again academic managers, connecting to new management challenges or reconnecting to former ones. The transition zones enable a fluidity for the academic manager's path (Bjørkeng et al., 2009; Bruni et al., 2007; Gherardi, 2019; Johnson, 2002; Lee & Amjadi, 2014; Loveday, 2021; Martin, 2022; Nicolini, 2003; Orlikowski & Scott, 2015; Winter, 2009). On the other hand, occupying the central intersection of the cauldron, dealing with oneself connects every category formerly developed, in which the humility, susceptibilities, emotions, and the role of family play crucial roles. These are the elements that encompass the food. It is necessary to remind their interplay with aspects such as dealing with structure, with power, with internal and external connections, which make up the broth in the cauldron, whose content we explore and detail in Chapter 4, the contextualizing elements.

This path and its features require university management several points of attention, assessment, and execution. A manager who is also academic has a crucial role in university management, because their hybrid features highly contribute to a university management that is complex, dynamic, and multifaceted. Firstly, it is important to have in mind that this path has a processual, complex, and circular logic. The entanglement of the elements needs special focus. Therefore, linear thinking is not suitable.

Secondly, the need for spaces, procedures, and qualifications in order to welcome the future and new academic managers, keeping in mind the bonus and onus of being a professor in structuring and executing some activities. Sometimes professors with good potential for management and leadership have not been contemplated and considered at university, including the related professors' awareness. We are supposed to stablish channels, procedures, and spaces to allow this identification. Furthermore, the first moments in management require support, mentoring, reflection, monitoring, and assessment. Moments of discussion and sharing are recommended.

Thirdly, we have to be aware of the nature of learning and knowing, mostly when we embrace the maturing process. There is a myriad of possibilities and opportunities related to learning, in which formal initiatives are only one little part, but with extreme relevance as basis and space for reflection, experience sharing, and discussion. We have to consider aspects such as mentoring, observation, informal moments, and experiences outside university for the accomplishment of practices, as well as the other publics that relate to academic managers. It is necessary to comprehend that physical spaces, systems, procedures, structures, interpersonal relationships, organizational climate, and power aspects contribute to the learning experience, both for the better and for the worse. Programs associated to management formation and qualification depend on a wider perspective on learning and knowing.

Lastly, disconnecting from management is a point university management needs to pay special attention to. Professors who leave management can present an array of reflections, doubts, and emotions that hinder their continuity at universities, mostly because they keep working with them. Procedures and structures of support and welcome are required, mainly for those who return only for teaching and researching.

Knowing is more than a list of tasks, observation of colleagues in the job, training, referrals to consultants, or any kind of prescription. Managers will act with their initial repertoire acquired through professional experiences and life. Learning to dialog, to make decisions, whether individually, with others' help/support or in collegiate spaces, to question, to listen to people from the social context, and to encompass informal learning opportunities are considered essential for the academic manager's path. Many of these elements can be developed in formal learning initiatives, taking into account the limitations of their nature in the academic managers' knowing and practices (Johnson, 2002; Loveday, 2021; Rodrigues & Villardi, 2017).

References

Bjørkeng, K., Clegg, S., & Pitsis, T. (2009). Becoming (a) practice. *Management Learning, 40*(2), 145–159. https://doi.org/10.1177/1350507608101226

Bruni, A., Gherardi, S., & Parolin, L. L. (2007). Knowing in a system of fragmented knowledge. *Mind, Culture, and Activity, 14*(1–2), 83–102. https://doi.org/10.1080/10749030701307754

Gherardi, S. (2009). Knowing and learning in practice-based studies: An introduction. *Learning Organization, 16*(5), 352–359. https://doi.org/10.1108/09696470910974144

Gherardi, S. (2019). *How to conduct a practice-based study: Problems and methods.* Edward Elgar Publishing.

Gherardi, S., & Miele, F. (2018). Knowledge management from a social perspective: The contribution of practice-based studies. In J. Syed, P. A. Murray, D. Hislop, & Y. Mouzughi (Eds.), *The Palgrave handbook of knowledge management* (pp. 151–176). Springer. https://doi.org/10.1007/978-3-319-71434-9_7

Johnson, R. (2002). Learning to manage the university: Tales of training and experience. *Higher Education Quarterly, 56*(1), 33–51. https://doi.org/10.1111/1468-2273.00201

Lee, C. F., & Amjadi, M. (2014). The role of materiality: Knowing through objects in work practice. *European Management Journal, 32*(5), 723–734. https://doi.org/10.1016/j.emj.2014.01.004

Loveday, V. (2021). 'Under attack': Responsibility, crisis and survival anxiety amongst manager-academics in UK universities. *The Sociological Review, 69*(5), 903–919. https://doi.org/10.1177/0038026121999209

Martin, Q. (2022). From faculty to administration: Preparing the next generation of academic leaders. *Perspectives: Policy and Practice in Higher Education, 26*(3), 109–114. https://doi.org/10.1080/13603108.2021.2016513

Nicolini, D. (2003). *Knowing in organizations: A practice-based approach.* Routledge. https://doi.org/10.4324/9781315290973

Orlikowski, W. J., & Scott, S. V. (2015). Exploring material-discursive practices. *Journal of Management Studies, 52*(5), 697–705. https://doi.org/10.1111/joms.12114

Rodrigues, A. C. A. L., & Villardi, B. Q. (2017). Teacher training for university management: An inductive analysis of the professors of the stricto sensu postgraduation from UFRRJ. *Revista Foco, 10*(2), 208–231. https://doi.org/10.28950/1981-223x_revistafocoadm/2017.v10i2.408

Winter, R. (2009). Academic manager or managed academic? Academic identity schisms in higher education. *Journal of Higher Education Policy and Management, 31*(2), 121–131. https://doi.org/10.1080/13600800902825835

Contextualizing Elements of Academic Managers' Knowing

Abstract In this chapter we explore the analytical category "Dealing with the nature of the academic and manager relationship". In the framework it is represented by the clay cauldron, the material that gives a special flavor to the broth in chemical transformation with food. We take into account elements such as teaching contributing to management and vice-versa, research contributing to management, and the weight of the interaction between manager and professor. Within this context, we conclude with opportunities, challenges, and guidelines regarding academic managers' development of skills, attitudes, and behaviors, emphasizing the importance of their role in university management.

Keywords Academic manager · Academic manager's path · Academic manager's knowing · Context

This chapter is focused on the contextualizing elements of academic managers' knowing. Looking at the cauldron, these elements make up the "Broth", in chemical transformation with food, which are the aspects developed in Chapter 3 and linked with the academic manager's path. We, therefore, explore the microcategories related to each analytical category, mentioned in Chapter 2, with regard to what we call the "Broth" in

© The Author(s), under exclusive license to Springer Nature Switzerland AG 2024
F. Larentis and C. S. Antonello, *Knowledge and Learning in Organizations*, https://doi.org/10.1007/978-3-031-61167-4_4

the cauldron: Dealing with structure and processes; Dealing with power; Dealing with external connections; Dealing with internal connections.

We highlight that the analytical categories which represent food are in interaction with each contextualizing element. For example, it means that the analytical category "Connecting to management" interacts with dealing with structure and processes, dealing with power, dealing with external connections, and dealing with internal connections. There are also shared elements between food and the broth. The culinary metaphor enables this conceptual feature.

4.1   Dealing with Structure and Processes

The first contextualizing element we explore is the analytical category Dealing with structure and processes. As mentioned in Chapter 2, this category involves hierarchical structures, bureaucracy levels, and the processes associated to communication, administrative routines, and decision taking. This analytical category embraces the microcategories Dealing with hierarchy and Dealing with processes.

Dealing with hierarchy considers the way in which the academic manager gets involved, faces and copes with the effects of centralization and the flow of decision-making, such as the level of dependence of employees on the manager in decision-making and the extent to which they are able to develop autonomy, as well as understanding and shaping the complementary and contradictory aspects between centralization and decentralization. Likewise, the effect of the hierarchical structure itself on the professional and personal lives of those involved. In this context, it has been mentioned how the academic manager must deal with employees with more technical knowledge and more time on the job, including in situations where they take advantage of the manager's lack of knowledge.

In the role of the hierarchical structure, it emerged from the field, mainly through observations, the degree to which the structure interferes with internal processes and external contacts, with bureaucratic aspects, which, in certain situations, serve as obstacles due to the way in which the hierarchy and its flows are established and the confusion with certain positions and their roles, especially when there are changes or the emergence of new departments or sectors. It is necessary to consider the effects of a culture of centralization at the university, which interferes with the decisions and behavior of academic managers and their teams. In addition, we draw attention to the effects of the configuration of the spaces set up for collegiate decisions on the decisions and actions of academic managers, such as the University Council. Finally, there are the interpersonal relationships that change because of hierarchical changes, which is also associated with power issues.

Regarding autonomy a coordinator commented that she does not like to say, "take care of this, do that". She would say: "observe, take ownership, stay in place to listen, allow yourself this time and then, if you need anything, talk to me". This coordinator also commented about some employees' passivity at taking decisions, waiting for their superiors, which is associated to a centralizing culture. On the other hand, with regard to centralization, a retired academic manager mentioned that at the same time as there was a complaint from the units about centralization in the rectory, there were also complaints from the rectory that the units had too much autonomy. According to him, these two situations are mutually exclusive, they can be complementary because both seemed to be partially correct.

Dealing with processes covers the level of clarity of processes, especially when communication channels are involved, as well as the way bureaucracy is operationalized, but also used in favor of some and against others. Some of the interviewees emphasized the difficulties in getting certain projects off the ground and implementing and executing them, since they must deal with unfinished actions and the demotivation that comes with this. This gave rise to what was referred to as a culture of complaining.

A campus director emphasizes the issue of lack of clarity about some processes and the interface that these processes have, which ends up generating a great deal of difficulty for the academic managers. A coordinator warns that the worst way to lose someone is to lose them and have them remain in the institution, in other words, by taking away all their motivation and initiative, although they have been lost, they remain at work.

4.2   Dealing with Power

As mentioned in Chapter 2, dealing with power encompasses aspects connected with the constitution of the capability and condition to influence and direct actions, behaviors, and interests. This analytical category is equivalent to the following microcategories: Dealing with the authority of the position, Meanings arising from physical spaces, Dealing with the contradictory and conflicts, and Dealing with the level of exposure.

Dealing with the authority of the position involves learning that is inherent to the power associated with certain assigned hierarchical positions in terms of management, which is also associated with leadership processes. In this regard, people were mentioned and perceived as having less power than they believe they have, in other words, a perception of authority that does not necessarily align with what is configured in terms of leadership. A knowledge area director argued that words are performative, they literally perform things. Remembering our positions we always must carefully scale what we are saying. Sometimes something that seemed like a huge problem ends up being minimized. In addition, a coordinator mentioned the situation of certain academic managers who are moved to other positions in order to be silenced.

Meanings arising from physical spaces have association with the way in which workrooms, their size, divisions, doors, furniture, equipment, and artifacts are representative of power relations and both the work and leadership styles of academic managers.

A former manager referred to the workplace as a "confessional", a space for listening similar to a classroom for listening to students. A knowledge area director mentioned that his workroom may generate more tension in certain situations, therefore causing him to go elsewhere to talk to increase informality, just as he praised the importance of leaving the door to his office open most of the time. According to him, a closed door can represent an impediment to frank relations.

Dealing with the contradictory and conflicts is presented in tensions and opportunities posed by differences of ideas, interests, and worldviews. This includes the way in which proposals and decisions appear rational due to the volume of information created and the production of knowledge that is inherent to a university. There are also times in which certain situations and demands are solemnly ignored, as mentioned by a coordinator, or when confrontation takes place. In this context, we have identified the importance of spaces and moments where contradiction takes place, decision-making takes place in a context of difficulty in dealing with conflicts and clashes, as well as actions and directions that give the impression of collective construction but are not.

A former academic manager who is currently a professor reinforces that living democratic processes within a university is fundamental, which represents a space where contradiction takes place or discussions can be held, in which suggestions are valued and intellectual potential is valued because a university is made up of brains.

A retired academic manager questions what the typical conflicts at university are. He answers that within the university there are three streams of thought, The first comprehends those who have a historical perspective of the university as an institution, in which knowledge is the center of everything. The second stream is related to those with a corporative vision, who consider mainly the professor's category. He calls the third stream functionalism, which is focused on results, mostly financial ones. According to him, the worst problem in the university is precisely this appearance of rationality where everyone who defends any kind of radical position is convinced that they are being fully rational.

In Dealing with the level of exposure, academic managers consist of their visibility based on the characteristics of their position, their decisions and actions and the extent to which they are considered a reference. Exposure is associated to the ability to occupy and expose oneself in certain spaces, such as meetings, and what it means for the academic manager to become further involved and their potential to influence, which includes dealing with the said and the unsaid, the art of not saying and understanding what is between the lines. In other words, the pros and cons of appearing and becoming more involved, which includes people who avoid exposing themselves to feel more protected and avoid situations in which they feel boycotted or ignored. We have also identified the condition of dealing with the loneliness of the position at certain times and in certain situations.

A former academic manager, who is currently retired, mentioned the positions that began to emerge in the last meetings of the university council, which had not been verbalized before and that were opposed to what had already been agreed and approved, by her team itself. During this period differences became clearer.

4.3 Dealing with External Connections

According to Chapter 2, Dealing with external connections considers the nature and scope of contacts between the university and its stakeholders. Amplitude and quality of external contacts, Dealing with students, graduates, and the regional community, and Dealing with organizations outside the region.

Amplitude and quality of external contacts embraces the extent of contacts between universities and their external stakeholders, as well as the characterization of these contacts, which consider the background and interest of those involved. We can consider the academic manager as a boundary spanner, the one who acts as an organization representative or interpreter of the external environment across organizational boundaries, therefore representing the most crucial vehicle for building and maintaining strong relationships (Araujo et al., 2003; Palmatier, 2008).

It was mentioned how much the external community, in all its groupings, cares about the actions and challenges of the university, which is of a community nature. Similarly, there were reports of how much is learned from external contacts, considering the way the university connects and adheres to the needs of the communities in which it is inserted. In this case the level and characteristics of the distance between the institution and the community can be perceived, including how the image and reputation of the academic manager in external connections is perceived. With these learnings, it was possible to expand the number of examples and references between the university and its stakeholders.

According to a knowledge area director, the whole university has learned a lot with external exchanges, in search of partnerships, in search of dialogue, by assessing possibilities and projects. It is a continuous learning process, and the university is supposed to be humble, with a conversation of collaboration and contribution.

In Dealing with students, graduates, and the regional community, we examine, the amplitude and quality of contacts with these publics. Students play a crucial role due to their connections to academic managers when teaching and researching as well as in situations where requirements and complaints are present. The other publics can provide work and income for the institution, in the form of courses, other services, and projects depending on the quality of the relationship between members of the university. In this sense, graduates can play a crucial role by assisting the activities of the academic manager when in contact with the community. On the other hand, a rectory's member mentioned the perception of parts of the community, such as entrepreneurs, who are afraid of the university, which may be associated with fear of the unknown, but also with the quality of the university's connections and deliveries in the past.

In this aspect, a campus director emphasizes the university's need to reach the community effectively, not just when the student takes the admission tests and enrolls. The university is not left out, it is one of those community bodies. The community, such as the alumni and entrepreneurs, helps with the projects technically, in practice with the projects, with the actions, with the university insertion, in the day-by-day, and in the classroom.

Dealing with organizations outside the region reflects the quality and breadth of contacts with organizations outside the region involved in the institution's activities and processes, especially research, innovation, and management processes, mostly universities, research institutions, governmental agencies, and companies. In this regard, we highlight the relationship with other national or international universities, especially in terms of management models and the development of partnerships, involving benchmarking activities through contacts and visits. Important examples are the multi-campus model inspired from a Canadian university (University of Montreal) and being part of a community universities consortium.

A retired academic manager emphasizes the importance of national and global partnerships. They reduce costs, open paths, open doors in an outstanding way in a short time.

4.4   DEALING WITH INTERNAL CONNECTIONS

Dealing with internal connections, as indicated in Chapter 2, embraces relationships inside the university, between the academic managers and their teams, the managers who do not have academic positions and other university departments. Relating to the teams, Dealing with non-academic managers, and Dealing with support sectors.

Relating to the teams is associated with the way academic managers deal and interact with their subordinates and realize their leadership role in the team, which can include other professors. We have identified aspects in the research such as the achievement of results contributing to teams' building and commitment, with the work being carried out and the results achieved together, the condition as a professor to obtain the engagement of the team, just as they obtain the engagement of the students in the classroom. This will depend on how academic managers deal with emotions, how they deal with the potential of employees, and how open they are to dialog, as well as to employees' warnings, due to their routine knowledge and experience.

The employees interviewed highlighted the openness to dialogue, which enables ease to talk about problems and mistakes, including the chance for the team to alert the academic manager to certain decisions, regardless of their work overload and multiplicity of activities. According to some of the academic managers interviewed, this openness was an element that allowed them to learn more about university management.

In this context, an employee reinforces the importance for the manager to see each person as a whole, as a professional along with their activities, where everyone as a team can contribute. The managers should clearly see what they expect from their team, what everyone can do together, change and improve.

Dealing with non-academic managers encompasses the characteristics and challenges of dealing with professionals at managerial level who do not have the role of professors, who hold different perceptions and world-views about how they conduct the university's operations and business. In this context, an interviewee mentioned the secondary role and importance of management at the university in the past. An example of this relationship is the nature of some of the non-academic managers' questions about the decisions of area and campus directors, to the point in which a campus director often sees herself as a luxury caretaker, due to the level of autonomy in certain decisions.

Another aspect is the questioning of the effectiveness of non-academic-managers assuming academic positions. According to a rectory's member, the peculiarities of university management and the experience as professors and researchers contribute for the academic managers' role.

Dealing with support sectors considers the quality and breadth of the academic managers' connections with administrative sectors that support both academic issues and other aspects of the university's operations, such as finance, marketing, legal, logistics, purchasing, property, and human resources. Based on the findings, we highlight the way in which the sense of urgency and the ability to understand the situation of problems in various sectors is presented, which are based on what is demanded of them, and how much conversation, coordination, and alignment linked to moments of tension are needed in order for certain projects and directions to be implemented.

In this sense, some employees connected to the academic manager, due to their technical knowledge, show certain levels of accommodation, question the manager's decisions, and put bureaucratic aspects as barriers to certain solutions. An important aspect in this regard is the way in which academic managers and support sectors manage to get closer to reduce the distance between the comprehension and interpretation of determined situations. In this regard, as the support sectors are located basically in the main university campus, a campus director mentions the need for support sectors to deeply know the institution as a whole, mainly its variety of structures and connections in the other campus.

4.5 DISCUSSION AND IMPLICATIONS

Academic manager's knowing is permeated by social, historical, emotional, sociomaterial, and power-related aspects. It is entangled with the multifaceted nature of the academic manager role, in which we take into account rationality as situational and contingent (Bjørkeng et al., 2009; Gherardi, 2019; Johnson, 2002; Loveday, 2021; Martin, 2022; Orlikowski & Scott, 2015; Rodrigues & Villardi, 2017; Winter, 2009). This is the reason the contextualizing elements are in interaction with the elements that constitute the academic manager's path. In other words, food is in chemical transformation with the broth.

Therefore, according to the findings, the importance of understanding the configuration of the academic manager's knowing became clear when we identified, from the connection to the disconnection to management, the interactions that take place between the individuals involved, at different hierarchical levels, internally and externally to the institution. We also must pay attention to people's backgrounds, emotional issues, aspects relating to politics and power, hierarchical structures, processes, the nature and the quality of the relationships, and sociomaterial aspects.

Dealing with structure and processes requires the academic managers' special attention to the nature and features of the university hierarchy, the bureaucratic aspects, and the way the processes are organized and structured. This attention is also needed when dealing with power and its elements, which are associated to authority dynamics, contradictory issues, conflicts, and levels of exposure. Structure, processes, and power issues are also in connection with the nature and idiosyncrasies of internal and external relationships, between academic managers and their teams, non-academic managers, support sectors, students, alumni, organizations, and communities. Moreover, the contextualizing elements also require consideration to sociomaterial aspects, when we contemplate the hierarchy per se, artifacts, documents, procedures, methodologies, physical spaces, and the definition of the roles' scopes.

These elements present important effects, and action, on academic managers' roles, practices, and knowing. They are not in the vacuum, they matter. Therefore, academic managers' qualification programs should consider the contextualizing elements in their structuring and execution, their effects, reactions, contingencies, and situated concerns, both in formal and informal learning angles.

For example, a program that considers the qualification of leadership capabilities to academic managers should encompass not only the elements needed to improve leaders' abilities and attitudes. Moreover, this program ought to take into account the aspects associated to the academic manager's path (connecting to management, maturing as a manager, and disconnecting from management), including pedagogical methodologies that amplify students' engagement during the program, in interactive spaces that enable more interaction, inspiration, reflection, and creativity. Nonetheless, this program also has to consider the aspects associated to the structural, relational, and power contexts leaders are supposed to deal with in order for them to comprehend deeply the time and space they decide, solve problems, execute activities, manage conflicts, discuss, interpret, collaborate, influence, articulate, have doubts about managing, and disconnect from management.

REFERENCES

Araujo, L., Dubois, A., & Gadde, L. (2003). The multiple boundaries of the Firm. *Journal of Management Studies, 40*(5), 1255–1277. https://doi.org/10.1111/1467-6486.00379

Bjørkeng, K., Clegg, S., & Pitsis, T. (2009). Becoming (a) practice. *Management Learning, 40*(2), 145–159. https://doi.org/10.1177/1350507608101226

Gherardi, S. (2019). *How to conduct a practice-based study: Problems and methods* (2nd ed.). Edward Elgar Publishing.

Johnson, R. (2002). Learning to manage the university: Tales of training and experience. *Higher Education Quarterly, 56*(1), 33–51. https://doi.org/10.1111/1468-2273.00201

Loveday, V. (2021). 'Under attack': Responsibility, crisis and survival anxiety amongst manager-academics in UK universities. *The Sociological Review, 69*(5), 903–919. https://doi.org/10.1177/0038026121999209

Martin, Q. (2022). From faculty to administration: Preparing the next generation of academic leaders. *Perspectives: Policy and Practice in Higher Education, 26*(3), 109–114. https://doi.org/10.1080/13603108.2021.2016513

Orlikowski, W. J., & Scott, S. V. (2015). Exploring material-discursive practices. *Journal of Management Studies, 52*(5), 697–705. https://doi.org/10.1111/joms.12114

Palmatier, R. W. (2008). *Relationship marketing*. Marketing Science Institute.

Rodrigues, A. C. A. L., & Villardi, B. Q. (2017). Teacher training for university management: An inductive analysis of the professors of the stricto sensu post-graduation from UFRRJ. *Revista Foco, 10*(2), 208–231. https://doi.org/10.28950/1981-223x_revistafocoadm/2017.v10i2.408

Winter, R. (2009). Academic manager or managed academic? Academic identity schisms in higher education. *Journal of Higher Education Policy and Management, 31*(2), 121–131. https://doi.org/10.1080/13600800902825835

Constituting Oneself as an Academic Manager: Nature, Opportunities, Challenges, and Guidelines

Abstract In this chapter we explore the analytical category "Dealing with the nature of the academic and manager relationship", which represents the clay cauldron in the framework, the element that gives a special flavor to the broth (contextualizing elements) in chemical transformation with food (academic manager's path). We take into account elements such as teaching contributing to management and vice-versa, research contributing to management, and the weight of the interaction between manager and professor. Within this context, we conclude by recommending some ways to identify opportunities, challenges, and initiatives regarding academic managers' constitution of skills, attitudes, and behaviors. We also present some guidelines associated to academic manager's knowing and learning.

Keywords Academic manager · Academic manager's path · Academic manager's knowing · Academic and manager relationship

This chapter is dedicated to explore and deepen the analytical category "Dealing with the nature of the academic and manager relationship". Looking at the cauldron, this aspect is the clay cauldron, a material that allows a special flavor to the broth (the contextualizing elements—Chapter 4) in chemical reactions with food (the academic manager's path—Chapter 3). We address the elements that constitute the peculiarities and challenges linked to the interplay between the practices of professor and manager.

We thus present the findings and implications related to the following microcategories concerning the analytical category, mentioned in Chapter 2: Teaching contributing to management; Management contributing to teaching; Researcher contributing to management; Weight of the interaction between manager and professor.

As a clay cauldron regarding the interaction and contributions between the roles and practices as manager and the roles as professor/researcher, this analytical category has been chosen to involve the other categories, since it represents what we consider the essence of the role of the academic manager, the one that maintains the academic identity at university management (Barbosa et al., 2018; Castro & Tomàs, 2011; Ésther, 2011).

As commented in Chapter 1, we emphasize that academic managers are supposed to handle a multiplicity of roles, activities, and relationships, internal and external, as well as the temporariness of the position, certain levels of managerial preparation, time concerns, and power issues (Barbosa et al., 2016a, 2016b, 2017; Broadbent, 2011; Dowling-Hetherington, 2014; Geschwind et al., 2019a; Martin, 2022; Rodrigues & Villardi, 2017; Silva, 2012; Silva & Cunha, 2015). It is necessary to highlight the fundamental role of the context, which emcompasses its interpersonal, political, and ethical concerns (Barbosa et al., 2016a, 2016b; Bessant & Mavin, 2016; Machovcová et al., 2019).

The first microcategory we explore is Teaching contributing to management. The findings have indicated that teaching classes are moments of decompression from management, in which the professor can even enter into a flow process, as highlighted by a coordinator. Teaching serves as a possibility to forget and disconnect from management problems for a while. According to him, the concept of flow, of doing what one does well, almost unconsciously, teaching as a fun moment, allows switching off and separating teaching and managing.

There is also the performance of classroom activities contributing to university management, in view of the importance of maintaining management contact with the front line, i.e. the students. It allows reducing the risks of decision-making because the classroom serves as a source of information and opportunities.

On the other hand, we have noticed elements belonging to the role of professor that feed management, mostly because teaching can help to perceive the role of human relations in management, enhanced by those who enjoy teaching, as well as the capacity for dialogue, the quicker ability of some teachers to assimilate information and the manager playing the role of teacher with employees, in the sense of corrections and realignments in documents and speeches and the possibility of developing a critical sense. An employee mentioned her relationship with a professor. She considers him very critical, thus making her more mature and helping her to reflect and to question.

In this case, an academic manager may be teaching for a few hours a semester or even not performing teaching tasks, which happens for example with some rectory's members. The identity as professors remains in the context of management, in events, meetings, discussions, conflicts, and decision taking, in which knowledge organization, communications, and explanations take place. In a nutshell, as a rectory's member commented, teaching has the potential to reduce the harshness of becoming a manager.

According to the findings concerning Management contributing to teaching, the activities as manager can make the professor fairer and more focused, depending on certain activities and tensions. A coordinator commented that management has made him calmer and fairer, in which the sense of justice improved as manager, therefore helping in the classroom, since he can realize the differences between students and how he treats them.

There is also the sensitivity that emerges in the relationship between management and teaching, such as a professor that manages the student relationship and retention at university during classes. Moreover, they expand the list of management experiences provided by their practices at university as material for the classroom, especially for those associated with management and business subjects. Another coordinator emphasizes that the fact of having experience in management allows the establishment of better relations between theory and practice, which helps bring examples more naturally, materializing concepts in hypothetical situations created in class. For her, management experience is also knowing that everything is a process.

Moreover, it has become clear that academic managers attach importance to management, but also that they have to deal with the belittling of being a manager, both from themselves and from others, a situation mentioned by a former academic manager and nowadays acting only as professor.

The microcategory Researcher contributing to management encompasses the master's and doctoral degrees contributing to management, not only to researching and teaching. We also have the movement toward bringing research studies closer to improving the university management processes and the creation of business units within the university, even with research with an initially only academic focus. In addition, the skills derived from research, especially for those academic managers who work in graduate programs, such as information gathering, data analysis, and systematization, have contributed to the qualification of management activities and processes. As mentioned by a rectory's member, she is able to categorize what he hears because she usually records and categorizes, due to her research skills, for example in meetings or even coming up with ideas. By systematizing, the meetings can become more productive and the discussions can be more focused.

Nonetheless, academic managers' anxiety is due to their understanding of the scenarios. According to the findings, some aspects, circumstances, and problems may be over-understood, due to the professors' experience in analyzing and organizing information, which may generate unnecessary levels of anxiety and concerns. An analytical ability can make it difficult to see in perspective, the bigger picture.

Regarding Weight of the interaction between manager and professor, we take into account the conflicts, dilemmas, anxieties, concerns, and opportunities based on the way the roles of manager and professor are connected. Some interviewees questioned what is more important, the academic or the manager? Are they mainly professors or managers? Does the manager come first or does the professor come first? Or are there times and circumstances when determined combinations are more evident?

A certain level of quality as a professor contributes to a certain level of quality as a manager, and vice-versa, which is intensified when we consider the multiplicity and overload of activities, as well as the tensions and choices when we look at the balance between the professor's priorities and the manager's priorities. These questions become more evident in a context in which the importance of management itself for the economic university sustainability is increasing, given the reduction in the number of students over time, in particular undergraduates, the changes of educational technology, and increased competition.

A coordinator emphasizes that everything she learns from her students reverberates in management. According to her, it is a very symbiotic marriage, there is an intersection, and it is very interesting to be on both sides. Teaching gives her some prerogatives that allow her to improve practices in management. The dark side is the overload of activities, since management is cruel, it is incredibly demanding.

A long-standing employee had the feeling that it was bad to have an academic manager as her superior, due to the lack of exclusive dedication to management. Nowadays she realizes it is interesting to be involved with an academic manager, because they can look at situations from a manager's point of view, and with their eyes in the classroom they can solve several problems more quickly. There is less time available, but on the other hand, they bring teaching and research experiences that often contribute to problem solving.

Dealing with the nature of the academic and manager relationship, as the material that allows a special flavor to food and the broth in the cauldron. The combination of these elements, the academic manager's path (Chapter 3), the contextualizing elements (Chapter 4), and the condition of the interplay between the academic and the manager (this chapter) presents several challenges, but also opportunities for university management. In the next section we deepen these challenges and opportunities, thus proposing some guidelines in order to improve academic managers' practices.

5.1 Academic Manager's Knowing: Helping to Identify Opportunities, Challenges, and Initiatives

The knowing-in-practice notion emphasizes the role of human action in complex organizational work and encompasses connection between individuals, groups, organizations, and institutions in situated contexts, in social structures that are both the production of human activities and their context (Bruni et al., 2007; Orlikowski, 2002; Scaratti et al., 2009). In this landscape, knowing, as stressed by Gherardi and Miele (2018), is a collective activity situated in work practices, in the fragmented, distributed, and continuous management landscape. Both the knowing-in-practice notion and the concept of knowing are emphasized by the multifaceted and complex features of universities.

In our study, knowing is configured in the interweaving and confluence of connecting to management, of maturing as a manager, of disconnecting from management, and of the individual dealing with oneself, in the interplay with dealing with structure and processes, with power, with internal and external connections. Together, these elements connect to the core of the relationship and balance between the academic and the manager.

The book's framework, in other words, the cauldron, is represented by a multiplicity of connections, confluences, and entanglements associated to the configuration of academic manager's knowing. This reinforces the importance of investigating higher education organizations and actors, given their political, structural, and professional contexts (Barbosa et al., 2016a, 2017; Geschwind et al., 2019a, 2019b; Gherardi, 2021; Silva, 2012).

It is necessary to remember that learning is associated with formal and informal activities and contexts, as highlighted by Deem and Johnson (2003) and Rodrigues and Villardi (2017). Moreover, we highlight a formation that encompasses management practices not only focused on what managers "do", but on the consequences of their "doing" as well, as indicated by Price et al. (2020), since responsible management is embraced in situated practices of ethics, sustainability, and responsibility.

In this regard, we consider opportunities as conditions, circumstances, trends, and directions that can benefit the academic manager's role and knowing. On the other hand, the challenges pertain to the difficulties, barriers, and threats associated with academic managers' formation. Both opportunities and challenges contribute to the creation of proposals and plans involving the organization and the execution of learning projects, programs, or systems and other associated initiatives, in order to qualify academic managers and change/reinforce their practices in a way that their roles are respected and strengthened. For us, academic managers are one of the most important agents that enable universities to fulfill their missions, in their dynamic and multifaceted contexts.

Thus, in order to ease the identification of opportunities, challenges, and initiatives related to the academic manager's knowing in a specific university, taking into consideration the theoretical panorama mentioned previously, we propose Table 5.1, that presents in the lines the elements associated to the academic manager's path (connecting to management, maturing as a manager, disconnecting from management, transitions zones and dealing with oneself) and in the columns the contextual-izing elements (dealing with structure and processes, dealing with power, dealing with external connections, and dealing with internal connections). An example we have mentioned at the end of Chapter 4 follows this ratio-nale. We understand that the book is not supposed to present specific guidelines due to the idiosyncrasies of each HEI, that is why we have created this table.

Our intention with this table is to contribute with discussions and reflections encompassing learning projects, programs, or systems. In the structure of the table, we do not indicate the relationship between the academic and the manager, the clay cauldron, since its nature pervades the interactions between the academic manager's path and the contextu-alizing elements.

Furthermore, we state that the microcategories we have identified can be applied to other university classifications besides a community one, which is our study field. Nonetheless, we recognize the need to assess the framework's suitability whenever the table is used, due to particular features and circumstances of a university and other HEI.

We emphasize that the learning projects, programs, and systems, including the consideration of learning spaces, should address the nature of knowing and learning we have mentioned in the previous chapters and in the beginning of this section, as well as the features of practices. In other words, our intention is not either to fragment initiatives and actions due to the structure of the table, or disregard the connections and inter-actions between the framework's elements. There is a processual and fluid logic in the framework we are supposed to respect. The table serves as a visual tool in order to make tangible the entanglements associated with the cauldron of knowing. In association with the tables, the creation of cognitive maps can help.

The table can be used in several ways. For example, in order to qualify new academic managers, connecting to management is a fundamental issue, regardless of the need to take into account the other components of the academic manager's path. In this case, we recommend filling in the table gaps that are associated with each contextualizing element, focusing on opportunities, challenges, and strategies of action. The table fulfilling varies according to each case, so it is not necessary to fill in every table cell.

We can also be interested in a specific contextualizing element, for example Leading with power. In this case, we suggest analyzing and

Table 5.1 Academic manager's knowing: identifying opportunities, challenges, and initiatives

			Dealing with structure and processes		Dealing with power			
Academic manager's path	Contextualizing elements Microcategories		Dealing with hierarchy	Dealing with processes	Dealing with the authority of the position	Meanings arising from physical spaces	Dealing with the contradic tory and conflicts	Dealing with the level of exposure
Connecting to management	*Connections before management*							
	Previous knowledge and experience							
	Interest in management							
	Memories of past actions							
	Connections with management							
Maturing as a manager	*Learning from amplitude*							
	Learning through mistakes							
	Learning through pain							
	Learning through problem solving							
	Dealing with data and their formats							
	Interacting with information systems							
	Interacting with management methodologies and tools							

Academic manager's path	Contextualizing elements	Dealing with structure and processes		Dealing with power			
	Microcategories	Dealing with hierarchy	Dealing with processes	Dealing with the authority of the position	Meanings arising from physical spaces	Dealing with the contradictory and conflicts	Dealing with the level of exposure
	Role of documents						
	Knowing through reflection						
	Memories of past actions						
	Reading contexts						
	Working with the diversity of activities						
	Working with time						
	Sharing and dialoguing						
	Articulating						
	Becoming a reference						
Disconnecting from management	*Concerns about succession*						
	Managing to detach						
	Dealing with the return to teaching						
Dealing with oneself	*Dealing with humility and susceptibilities*						
	Dealing with emotions						
Transitions Zones	*Role of the family*						
	From connection to maturation						
	From maturation to disconnection						
	From disconnection to future						
	(re)connections						

(continued)

Table 5.1 (continued)

Academic manager's path	Contextualizing elements / Microcategories	Dealing with external connections			Dealing with internal connections		
		Amplitude and quality of external contacts	Dealing with students, graduates and the regional community	Dealing with organizations outside the region	Relating to the teams	Dealing with non-academic managers	Dealing with support sectors
Connecting to management	*Connections before management*						
	Previous knowledge and experience						
	Interest in management						
	Memories of past actions						
	Connections with management						
Maturing as a manager	*Learning from amplitude*						
	Learning through mistakes						
	Learning through pain						
	Learning through problem solving						
	Dealing with data and their formats						
	Interacting with information systems						
	Interacting with management						
	methodologies and tools						
	Role of documents						
	Knowing through reflection						

Academic manager's path	Microcategories	Contextualizing elements	Dealing with external connections			Dealing with internal connections		
			Amplitude and quality of external contacts	Dealing with students, graduates and the regional community	Dealing with organiza tions outside the region	Relating to the teams	Dealing with non-academic managers	Dealing with support sectors
	Memories of past actions							
	Reading contexts							
	Working with the diversity of activities							
	Working with time							
	Sharing and dialoguing							
	Articulating							
	Becoming a reference							
Disconnecting from management	*Concerns about succession*							
	Managing to detach							
	Dealing with the return to teaching							
Dealing with oneself	*Dealing with humility and susceptibilities*							
	Dealing with emotions							
Transitions Zones	*Role of the family*							
	From connection to maturation							
	From maturation to disconnection							
	From disconnection to future (re)connections							

assessing each element associated with the academic manager's path with the focus on power issues. It is also important to consider, in a complementary way, the interplay between this contextualizing element and the other. A focus on power issues does not mean disregarding the other contextualizing elements, but a special look at power issues.

5.2   Academic Manager's Knowing: Recommending Some Guidelines

In Sect. 5.1 we present a tool (table) that allows the identification of opportunities, challenges, and initiatives by connecting the academic manager's path (food) and the contextualizing elements (the broth). Nonetheless, by using this tool we recommend some guidelines that we present as follows.

Firstly, knowing is a collective activity situated in work practices. With this focus, we talk about managing instead of management. Both knowing and managing are conceived as processes that emerge from and are incorporated in situated practices. When we consider the university context, we encompass a myriad of features, specificities, challenges, and initiatives in a kind of organization that is knowledge-intensive.

Secondly, academic managers' knowing is configured through the interaction between formal and informal learning possibilities, by the constitution of practices. In such aspect, we are supposed to take into account a holistic and collective view of learning, as we can realize when looking at the microcategories our findings support, mainly by considering the academic manager's path, from connecting to management to disconnecting to management, in interplay with the contextualizing elements. In a nutshell, knowing is configured through discussions, dialogues, previous experiences and qualification, reflections, data analyses, recordings, internal and external relationships, articulations, influences, conflicts, pain, problem solving, and emotions. We have a context that depends on structural, power, social, and relational aspects. In this perspective, we also have to keep in mind the physical spaces for learning and the learning management systems we can use.

Third, sociomaterial aspects matter. In our findings, we have microcategories that evidence this importance, such as dealing with data, information systems, management tools, documents, organizational structures, and physical spaces. The increasing role of technology in education reinforces this aspect.

Fourthly, moments of formal learning provide a basis for dialogue, discussions, practice sharing, and reflections, throughout the stages of the academic manager's path, according to the university qualification purposes. There are even several possibilities to allow learning, learning programs, or courses defining some theoretical and practical directions. We have to pay attention to the directions chosen in order to provide this basis.

This includes the consideration of professors' features that can generate opportunities but also barriers to managers' formation, such as emotional aspects. Furthermore, we add the opportunities a university has to provide for the formation and qualification that embraces several themes of its teaching body. For a lifelong learning perspective, these courses provide the end of the beginning, not the beginning of the end.

Fifth, the academic manager's path deserves special attention. This attention does not only refer to qualification processes, but also to the inclusion of policies that embrace the management connection, maturing as a manager and the management disconnection, as well as the circular logic that involves this path, including the transition zones. Moreover, the cauldron logic is supposed to be addressed, in which we enlighten the contextualizing moments (the broth) and the academic and manager relationship (the clay cauldron) in connection with the path (food).

Besides being prepared (on a certain level) to begin managing, academic managers are supposed to be prepared to leave management and also to return to management. In this case, mentoring programs play an essential role, since they involve management newcomers, which encompasses the legitimate peripheral participation (LPP). LPP encourages a focus that enables newcomers to participate actively and legitimately in their performance of tasks, even if their contributions may be limited (Gherardi & Miele, 2018; Lave & Wenger, 1991). In this case, the more experienced managers as well as those that leave management can assume as mentors. Another issue is the significance of identifying and encouraging professors with potential to assume management positions.

Sixth, it is necessary to consider the assessment of learning, including a rationale that encompasses the concepts of knowing, practice, and knowing-in-practice. The assessments are supposed to be diverse, processual, and carried out in various moments because knowing in the context of universities is gradual, dependent on experiences, paths, social interactions, sociomaterial aspects, and power issues.

Lastly, we should be prepared to handle some levels of professors' resistance in order to be qualified. A professor who is an expert in a certain area may not be aware of the need to improve their managerial capabilities. Sometimes we need to show the obvious. Being a professor does not guarantee a full comprehension of facts. In this aspect, in order to generate professors' engagement for learning it is important to consider the process of giving sense and breaking sense, in other words, sensegiving and sensebreaking in the context of sensemaking. Sensegiving encompasses the attempt to influence others' sensemaking toward a preferred redefinition of organizational reality, while sensebreaking embraces destruction of meaning, since it occurs when sensemaking is interrupted by divergent evidence (Gioia & Chittipeddi, 1991; Maitlis & Christianson, 2014; Moon et al., 2017; Weick, 1995).

Therefore, we highlight these guidelines that pertain to the nature of knowing and learning, sociomaterial aspects, the academic manager's path, and the assessment of learning and engagement. Taking them into consideration shall be fruitful for university management, due to the relevance of the academic manager's knowing, its complexity, diversity, and situatedness.

References

Barbosa, M. A. C., Matos, F. R. N., Mendonça, J. R. C., Paiva, K. C. M., & Cassundé, F. R. de S. A. (2017). The role of manager: Perceptions from academic managers of a Brazilian Federal University. *Education Policy Analysis Archives, 25.* https://doi.org/10.14507/epaa.25.2388

Barbosa, M. A. C., Mendonça, J. R. C., & Cassundé, F. R. S. A. (2016a). The interaction between the role of academic-manager and managerial competences: Perceptions of teachers from a federal university. *Organizações em Contexto, 12*(23), 287–325.

Barbosa, M. A. C., Mendonça, J. R. C., & Cassundé, F. R. S. A. (2016b). Managerial competences (expected versus perceived) of academic managers of federal higher education institution: Perceptions of teachers from a federal university. *Administração: Ensino e Pesquisa, 17*(3), 439–473. https://doi.org/10.13058/raep.2016.V17n3.344

Barbosa, M. A. C., Paiva, K. C. M., & Mendonça, J. R. C. (2018). Social role and professional and managerial competences of higher education professor: Similarities between the constructs and research perspectives. *Organizações & Sociedade, 25*(84), 100–121. https://doi.org/10.1590/1984-9240846

Bessant, C., & Mavin, S. (2016). Neglected on the front line: Tensions and challenges for the first-line manager-academic role in UK business schools. *Journal of Management Development, 35*(7), 916–929. https://doi.org/10. 1108/JMD-09-2014-0105

Broadbent, J. (2011). Discourses of control, managing the boundaries. *The British Accounting Review, 43*(4), 264–277. https://doi.org/10.1016/j.bar. 2011.08.003

Bruni, A., Gherardi, S., & Parolin, L. L. (2007). Knowing in a system of fragmented knowledge. *Mind, Culture, and Activity, 14*(1–2), 83–102. https:// doi.org/10.1080/10749030701307754

Castro, D., & Tomàs, M. (2011). Development of manager-academics at institutions of higher education in Catalonia. *Higher Education Quarterly, 65*(3), 290–307. https://doi.org/10.1111/j.1468-2273.2011.00490.x

Clegg, S. (2003). Learning and teaching policies in higher education: Mediations and contradictions of practice. *British Educational Research Journal, 29*(6), 803–819. https://doi.org/10.1080/0141192032000137312

Deem, R., & Johnson, R. (2003). Risking the university? Learning to be a manager-academic in UK universities. *Sociological Research Online, 8*(3), 1–15. https://doi.org/10.5153/sro.819

Dowling-Hetherington, L. (2014). The changing demands of academic life in Ireland. *International Journal of Educational Management, 28*, 141–151. https://doi.org/10.1108/IJEM-02-2013-0021

Ésther, A. B. (2011). The managerial competencies of the deans of federal universities in Minas Gerais: The perception of top management. *Cadernos EBAPE.BR, 9*, 648–667. https://doi.org/10.1590/S1679-395120110006 00011

Frenkel, S. J. (2021). Embedded in two worlds: The university academic manager's work, identity and social relations. *Educational Management Administration & Leadership*, 1–18. https://doi.org/10.1177/174114322 11027643

Geschwind, L., Aarrevaara, T., Berg, L. N., & Lind, J. K. (2019a). The changing roles of academic leaders: Decision-making, power, and performance. In R. Pinheiro, L. Geschwind, H. F. Hansen, & K. Pulkkinen (Eds.), *Reforms, organizational change and performance in higher education: A comparative account from the Nordic countries* (pp. 181–210). Springer Nature. https://doi.org/ 10.1007/978-3-030-11738-2_6

Geschwind, L., Kekäle, J., Pinheiro, R., & Sørensen, M. P. (2019b). Responsible universities in context. In M. P. Sørensen, L. Geschwind, J. Kekäle, & R. Pinheiro (Eds.), *The responsible university: Exploring the nordic context and beyond* (pp. 3–29). Springer Nature. https://doi.org/10.1007/978-3-030-25646-3_1

Gherardi, S. (2019). *How to conduct a practice-based study: Problems and methods.* Edward Elgar Publishing.

Gherardi, S. (2021). A posthumanist epistemology of practice. In C. Neesham (Ed.), *Handbook of philosophy of management, handbooks in philosophy* (pp. 1–22). Springer. https://doi.org/10.1007/978-3-319-48352-8_53-1

Gherardi, S., & Miele, F. (2018). Knowledge management from a social perspective: The contribution of practice-based studies. In J. Syed, P. A. Murray, D. Hislop, & Y. Mouzughi (Eds.), *The Palgrave handbook of knowledge management* (pp. 151–176). Springer. https://doi.org/10.1007/978-3-319-714 34-9_7

Gioia, D. A., & Chittipeddi, K. (1991). Sensemaking and sensegiving in strategic change initiation. *Strategic Management Journal, 12*(6), 433–448. https://doi.org/10.1002/smj.4250120604

Johnson, R. (2002). Learning to manage the university: Tales of training and experience. *Higher Education Quarterly, 56*(1), 33–51. https://doi.org/10.1111/1468-2273.00201

Lave, J., & Wenger, E. (1991). *Situated learning: Legitimate peripheral participation.* Cambridge University Press.

Machovcová, K., Zábrodská, K., & Mudrák, J. (2019). Department heads negotiating emerging managerialism: The Central Eastern European context. *Educational Management Administration & Leadership, 47*(5), 712–729. https://doi.org/10.1177/1741143217753193

Maitlis, S., & Christianson, M. (2014). Sensemaking in organizations: Taking stock and moving forward. *The Academy of Management Annals, 8*(1), 57–125. https://doi.org/10.5465/19416520.2014.873177

Martin, Q. (2022). From faculty to administration: preparing the next generation of academic leaders. *Perspectives: Policy and Practice in Higher Education, 26*(3), 109–114. https://doi.org/10.1080/13603108.2021.2016513.

Moon, H., Ruona, W., & Valentine, T. (2017). Organizational strategic learning capability: Exploring the dimensions. *European Journal of Training and Development, 41*(3), 222–240. https://doi.org/10.1108/EJTD-08-2016-0061

Orlikowski, W. J. (2002). Knowing in practice: Enacting a collective capability in distributed organizing. *Organization Science, 13*(3), 249–273. https://doi.org/10.1287/orsc.13.3.249.2776

Orlikowski, W. J., & Scott, S. V. (2015). Exploring material-discursive practices. *Journal of Management Studies, 52*(5), 697–705. https://doi.org/10.1111/joms.12114

Price, O. M., Gherardi, S., & Manidis, M. (2020). Enacting responsible management: A practice-based perspective. In O. Laasch, et al. (Eds.), *Research handbook of responsible management* (pp. 392–409). Edward Elgar Publishing. https://doi.org/10.4337/9781788971966.00035

Protasio, M., & Tauchen, G. (2021). The academic manager in the coordination of undergraduate courses: An integrative review. *Poíesis Pedagógica, 19.* https://doi.org/10.5216/rppoi.v19.70779

Rodrigues, A. C. A. L., & Villardi, B. Q. (2017). Teacher training for university management: An inductive analysis of the professors of the stricto sensu postgraduation from UFRRJ. *Revista Foco, 10*(2), 208–231. https://doi.org/10.28950/1981-223x_revistafocoadm/2017.v10i2.408

Scaratti, G., Gorli, M., & Ripamonti, S. (2009). The power of professionally situated practice analysis in redesigning organizations. *Journal of Workplace Learning, 21*(7), 538–554. https://doi.org/10.1108/13665620910985531

Silva, F. M. V. (2012). The transition to university management: The meaning of interpersonal relationships. *Revista de Administração FACES Journal, 11*(4), 72–91.

Silva, F. M. V., & Cunha, C. J. C. (2015). Be leaving university manager: The interpesonal relationship. *Diálogo e Interação, 9*(1). https://doi.org/10.1590/1980-265X-TCE-2019-0057

Weick, K. E. (1995). *Sensemaking in organizations.* Sage.

CHAPTER 6

Concluding Remarks

Abstract Academic manager is the one who performs a role as manager without abandoning their teaching identity. In the light of the knowing-in-practice notion, academic manager's knowing is constituted by their management path, entangled with a situated university context dependent on social, structural, and power issues. We conclude this book by discussing and reinforcing the academic managers' role and their challenges, as well as by highlighting the framework we have analyzed and deepened, the cauldron of knowing of the academic manager.

Keywords Academic manager · Academic manager's path · Academic manager's knowing · Cauldron of knowing

Human activities take place as elements of organized and interconnected sets of activities (Schatzki, 2018). Learning is a socially configured process of positioning and providing participants with different resources and possibilities, which occurs in historical contexts interspersed with power relations (Alkemeyer & Buschmann, 2017; Nicolini, 2012). In this scenario, professional knowing, embodied in the workplace, is contextual: it is anchored in the sociomaterial relations of a specific organization, in which practice is a collective doing situated and imbued with knowing (Gherardi, 2015).

© The Author(s), under exclusive license to Springer Nature
Switzerland AG 2024
F. Larentis and C. S. Antonello, *Knowledge and Learning in Organizations*, https://doi.org/10.1007/978-3-031-61167-4_6

This book has explored academic managers' knowing, by deepening their features and conditions. By focusing on the findings of a research carried out in a community university located in southern Brazil, we have analyzed what we named as Cauldron of Knowing of the Academic Manager, which was inspired by a culinary metaphor. By resuming the main findings, we have identified that academic managers' knowing is configured in the interaction, entanglement, and confluence of connecting to management, maturing as a manager, disconnecting from management, and individuals dealing with themselves, with the broth that comes from dealing with structure and processes, dealing with power, dealing with internal, and dealing external connections.

All these aspects together establish a connection with dealing with the nature of the academic and manager relationship. In metaphorical terms, we have the chemical reactions occurring with food (academic manager path) and the broth (contextualizing elements), thus acquiring a different flavor due to the material characteristics of a cauldron, in other words the nature of the academic and manager relationship. Therefore, we evince a cauldron of multiple connections, entanglements, and confluences in the configuration of the academic manager's knowing.

By bringing together the conceptual elements of practice and knowing-in-practice with the roles and attributions of the academic manager, we can reaffirm, based on the findings and the discussions, that there is no division between knowing and doing, since the phenomenon of learning in organizations is processual, social, and situated in practices (Antonello & Godoy, 2010; Chia, 2017; Cuel, 2020; Durante et al., 2019; Elkjaer, 2022; Gherardi, 2006, 2015, 2019; Hopwood, 2014; Nicolini et al., 2003; Price et al., 2020).

This is especially significant when we address the academic manager's role and their importance to university management. Academic managers maintain their teaching and researching identity, even when they do not teach classes or are fully engaged in management. Within their management practices they deploy capabilities to communicate, to speak, to organize and synthesize information and knowledge, to dialogue, to build lectures, to analyze data, to keep attention, and to inspire. On the other hand, such abilities may appear as barriers to determined management activities and practices. The academic manager is challenged to balance the time to dialog, the time to decide, and the time to execute, since we can have differences between the managing time and the teaching and researching times.

Therefore, we have a multifaceted and complex role, just like universities are. Universities are made to last, their purposes and missions are essential for more innovative, prosperous, and fairer societies. So, only short-term visions are troubling. These are the main reasons the academic manager is fundamental to university management. They have cons, but also pros, like any occupation or profession. Their experiences and history associated with university knowledge, learning, and knowing, which encompass all the elements of the cauldron, may generate more responsible and sustainable management practices. As boundary spanners, they impact on a myriad of interpersonal relationships, both internal and external. As agents of change, they deal with conflicts, contradictions, political aspects, and structural concerns.

Nonetheless, academic managers have to keep in mind and meet the need for formation and qualification, in order to improve their management capabilities, in a lifelong learning perspective, as well as their resilience in more and more dynamic and complex times. This perspective includes the encouragement of future university leaders. These are fundamental aspects for the sustainability of universities, in the economic, social, and environmental realms.

Knowledge is not something that people have only in their minds, but instead it is what they do together (Gherardi, 2006, 2019; Hopwood, 2014; Nicolini, 2012). Moreover, knowing and managing are conceived as processes that emerge from and are engendered in situated practices (Gherardi & Miele, 2018). Hence, the knowing-in-practice notion has provided us with a very suitable lens in order to comprehend the academic manager's knowing. With this book, we reinforce the importance of interpersonal relationships, power and political issues, sociomaterial aspects, trajectories, and the situated university contexts, in connection and entanglement.

References

Alkemeyer, T., & Buschmann, N. (2017). Learning in and across practices. In A. Hui, T. Schatzki, & E. Shove (Eds.), *The nexus of practices: Connections, constellations and practitioners* (pp. 8–23). Routledge.

Antonello, C. S., & Godoy, A. S. (2010). The crossroads of organizational learning: A multiparadigmatic view. *Revista de Administração Contemporânea, 14*, 310–332. https://doi.org/10.1590/S1415-65552010000200008

Chia, R. (2017). A process-philosophical understanding of organizational learning as "wayfinding" process, practices and sensitivity to environmental affordances. *The Learning Organization, 24*(2), 107–118. https://doi.org/10.1108/TLO-11-2016-0083

Cuel, R. (2020). A journey of learning organization in social science: Interview with Silvia Gherardi. *Learning Organization, 27*(5), 455–461. https://doi.org/10.1108/TLO-02-2020-0031

Durante, D. G., et al. (2019). Organizational learning in practice-based studies approach: Review of scientific production. *Revista de Administração Mackenzie, 20*(2), 1–27. https://doi.org/10.1590/1678-6971/eRA MG190131

Elkjaer, B. (2022). Taking stock of "Organizational Learning": Looking back and moving forward. *Management Learning, 53*(3), 582–604. https://doi.org/10.1177/13505076211049599

Gherardi, S. (2006). Organizational knowledge: The texture of workplace learning. *Scandinavian Journal of Management, 23*(2). https://doi.org/10.1016/j.scaman.2007.03.001

Gherardi, S. (2015). Why Kurt Wolff matters for a practice-based perspective of sensible knowledge in ethnography. *Journal of Organizational Ethnography, 4*(1), 117–131.

Gherardi, S. (2019). *How to conduct a practice-based study: Problems and methods.* Edward Elgar Publishing.

Gherardi, S., & Miele, F. (2018). Knowledge management from a social perspective: The contribution of practice-based studies. In J. Syed, P. A. Murray, D. Hislop, & Y. Mouzughi (Eds.), *The Palgrave handbook of knowledge management* (pp. 151–176). Springer. https://doi.org/10.1007/978-3-319-714 34-9_7

Hopwood, N. (2014). Four essential dimensions of workplace learning. *Journal of Workplace Learning, 26*(6/7), 349–363. https://doi.org/10.1108/JWL-09-2013-0069

Nicolini, D. (2012). *Practice theory, work & organization.* Oxford University Press.

Nicolini, D., Gherardi, S., & Yanow, D. (2003). Introduction: Toward a practice-based view of knowing and learning in organizations. In D. Nicolini, S. Gherardi, & D. Yanow (Eds.), *Knowing in organizations: A practice-based approach* (pp. 3–31). M. E. Sharpe. https://doi.org/10.4324/978131529 0973

Price, O. M., Gherardi, S., & Manidis, M. (2020). Enacting responsible management: A practice-based perspective. In O. Laasch, et al (Eds.), *Research handbook of responsible management* (pp. 392–409). Edward Elgar Publishing. https://doi.org/10.4337/9781788971966.00035

Schatzki, T. (2018). On practice theory, or what's practices got to do (got to do) with it? In C. Edwards-Groves, P. Grootenboer, & J. Wilkinson (Eds.), *Education in an era of schooling: Critical perspectives of educational practice and action research* (pp. 151–165). Springer.

Index

© The Editor(s) (if applicable) and The Author(s), under exclusive license to Springer Nature Switzerland AG 2024
F. Larentis and C. S. Antonello, *Knowledge and Learning in Organizations*, https://doi.org/10.1007/978-3-031-61167-4

GPSR Compliance

The European Union's (EU) General Product Safety Regulation (GPSR) is a set of rules that requires consumer products to be safe and our obligations to ensure this.

If you have any concerns about our products, you can contact us on ProductSafety@springernature.com

In case Publisher is established outside the EU, the EU authorized representative is:

Springer Nature Customer Service Center GmbH
Europaplatz 3
69115 Heidelberg, Germany

The manufacturer's authorised representative in the EU is Springer
Nature Customer Service Centre GmbH, Europaplatz 3, 69115 Heidelberg,
Germany. If you have any concerns regarding our products, please
contact ProductSafety@springernature.com

Printed and bound by CPI Group (UK) Ltd, Croydon, CR0 4YY

29/04/2026

02099531-0002